NEW IDEAS ON POPULATION

Also in

REPRINTS OF ECONOMIC CLASSICS

By ALEXANDER H. EVERETT

AMERICA [1827]

NEW IDEAS

ON

POPULATION

WITH

REMARKS ON THE THEORIES

OF

MALTHUS AND GODWIN

BY

ALEXANDER H. EVERETT

[1826]

With The Addition Of
The Correspondence Between Everett And George
Tucker On The Malthusian Theory, Published
In *The Democratic Review* For 1845 & 1847

REPRINTS OF ECONOMIC CLASSICS

AUGUSTUS M. KELLEY · PUBLISHERS
NEW YORK 1970

First Edition 1826

(Boston: Cummings, Hilliard & Company, 1826)

Reprinted 1970 by

AUGUSTUS M. KELLEY · PUBLISHERS

REPRINTS OF ECONOMIC CLASSICS

New York   New York   10001

· · · · · · · · ·

I S B N   0 678 00276 2

L C N   65 26364

· · · · · · · · · ·

PRINTED IN THE UNITED STATES OF AMERICA
by SENTRY PRESS, NEW YORK, N. Y. 10019

NEW IDEAS

ON

POPULATION:

WITH

REMARKS ON THE THEORIES

OF

MALTHUS AND GODWIN.

SECOND EDITION.

To which is prefixed

A NEW PREFACE,

CONTAINING

A BRIEF EXAMINATION OF THE OPINIONS OF MM. SAY
AND SISMONDI ON THE SAME SUBJECT.

By ALEXANDER H. EVERETT, A.A.S.

Minister Plenipotentiary of the United States of America at the Court of Spain.

BOSTON:

CUMMINGS, HILLIARD AND COMPANY.

1826.

CONTENTS.

PREFACE

———◆———

I have given the epithet *new* to the opinions maintained in the following little work, because they differ from those that are generally received, and not because they have never been suggested before. To this latter character, they have no pretensions; as they coincide in substance with the sentiments of the world at large, ,and of the most distinguished philosophers and legislators of all ages and nations. It has never been doubted, until very recently, that the increase of population was a symptom and a cause of public prosperity; and this is, in general terms, the principle which I have endeavored to establish. It was reserved for an English writer of the present day to produce temporarily a pretty extensive revolution in the public opinion upon this subject; and to convince most of the persons who take an interest in politi-

cal science, that the doctrines they had hitherto
received as sound, were not only false, but directly
opposed to the truth, and that the increase of
population, instead of being a cause and an indica-
tion of public prosperity, was on the contrary the
real and only source of all the evil we suffer.
This startling paradox, was supported by an argument, assuming the form without having in any
degree the character of a mathematical demonstration ; and by a strange caprice of public opinion,
was received at once with almost universal favor,
and has now maintained its ground for nearly
thirty years. The popularity of the system was
owing in part to its connexion with the political
events of the time when it appeared, the nature
of which is briefly stated in the first chapter of
the following work. But after making all proper
allowance for this circumstance, the remarkable
success which it met with, furnishes a singular
example of the truth of the Roman saying—
that books have their fortunes as well as men:
habent et sua fata libelli. Few persons, however,
think for themselves on points of abstract science ;
and two or three imposing names, representing
perhaps, in particular cases, judgments that are
hastily formed, will yet lead captive the under-

standings of a whole generation. A survey of
the received opinions of this and all other ages,
would indeed almost tempt one to suppose that
the world in adopting its articles of faith in matters
of science, proceeds upon the celebrated scheme
of one of the christian fathers and only admits
what it knows to be impossible.

The author of the paradox in question, deduces
from it among other conclusions that of the necessity of great foresight and prudence in contracting
marriages ; and thus far at least his practical
advice is sound, whatever may be thought of his
theories. There is no great danger that prudential
considerations will ever prevail over the suggestions of the social instinct, to a degree that shall
be dangerous to the welfare of society. But,
when Mr. Malthus deduces from his principles the
further conclusions, that public establishments for
the relief of the poor, the infirm, and the aged,
are positively injurious ; that private charity is a
merely imaginary virtue ; that the widest destruction of human life causes no real injury to society ;
and that all attempts to increase the happiness
of man by the improvement of existing political
institutions are hopeless and visionary ; when I say,
he advances these appalling propositions as just

deductions from his theory, and when it appears in fact that they do naturally follow from it, it becomes a matter of no little interest, even in mere speculation, to ascertain whether the theory be true, and all our best and noblest natural sentiments consequently false and deceptive ; or rather rejecting this idea, which cannot indeed be admitted for a moment, even as a supposition, to point out the errors in an argument, which has seduced for the last twenty or thirty years so many of the wisest heads in Europe and America.

This is the task that I have endeavored to execute, however imperfectly, in the little tract which is now again offered to the public. When I first published it two years ago in England and America, I was somewhat diffident about the correctness of my principles. I have since had the pleasure to find them confirmed by the approbation of many persons in whose judgment I place great confidence ; and my own subsequent reflections and researches have satisfied me, as far as I have a right to trust any conclusion of my own, that they are true. I therefore submit them to the public again, with less hesitation than I did at first ; and only regret that I have not been able to develope and illustrate them in a manner better suited to this great interest and importance. I shall be highly gratified on every account, should they be finally sanctioned by the favorable opinion of the American people.

The paradoxes of Mr. Malthus have not obtained upon the Continent of Europe the same degree of currency as in England, but have nevertheless been adopted by some of the most distinguished French philosophers. Mr. Say in particular, who has placed himself in public estimation at the head of the present race of writers on political economy, has lent the weight of his high authority to these opinions, although, as it seems to me, they stand in direct opposition with principles to which he attaches the greatest importance, and which he has defended with success against the attacks of Mr. Malthus himself. I shall take advantage of the present occasion to offer a few remarks upon the part of Mr. Say's justly celebrated treatise, in which he examines this subject.

The eleventh chapter of the second book of this treatise is devoted to the consideration of population as connected with political economy ; and contains in a very abridged form an exposition of some of the leading principles of the theory of Mr. Malthus. I cannot but think that the

author must have adopted them rather hastily, and
without a very thorough examination ; not only
because he has added no new matter of his own
in support of them, which a writer of so much
talent would hardly have failed to do—if he had
appropriated them to himself by sufficient investi-
gation and reflection ; but because among his
remarks upon the subject, he has introduced some
which are at variance with the theory, and which
he could not of course have made, if he had
thoroughly considered it in all its bearings. The
system of Malthus rests, as I have shewn in the
following work, on the supposition that it is
impossible for any given portion of the human
race to subsist, except upon the productions of the
very soil they occupy. Deny this, and his whole
fabric of mathematical demonstration falls to the
ground at once. But Mr. Say had evidently not
studied the theory sufficiently to perceive, that it
involves this supposition, since in the chapter
which is devoted to the exposition of it, he
remarks repeatedly that the inhabitants of many
countries are supported by supplies brought from
abroad.

'The means of subsistence,' says he, 'are not
always the direct products of the soil. They are

procured by commerce as well as agriculture ; and many countries support more inhabitants than could subsist upon their immediate productions.'* This single observation refutes satisfactorily the main argument, supported throughout the chapter, and it is repeated in substance several times. Thus the author remarks that, 'commerce, and especially foreign commerce, by facilitating exchanges even with distant countries, furnishes additional supplies of provisions, as well as many other articles.'† Again, 'the enormous amount of the products of industry in England permits the inhabitants of that country to increase to a much greater number than the soil would support;' and finally, 'there are seve- ral small states of which the whole territory would not furnish subsistence for one of the suburbs of the capital.'‡ It is evident from these and other obser-

* Les denrées alimentaires ne sont pas toutes des produits du sol ; on se les procure par le commerce aussi bien que par l'agriculture, et il y a plusieures contrées qui nourrissent bien plus d'habitans que n'en peuvent alimenter les produits de leurs terres.

† Le commerce et surtout le commerce maritime, facilitant les échanges et meme les échanges lointains, permet de se procurer des denrées alimentaires ainsi que beaucoup d'autres produits.

‡ La masse enorme de productions (en Angleterre,) permet à ce peuple de se multiplier au dela du nombre que le sol peut nourrir—; and finally, Il y a plusieurs petits Etats dont le territoire seul ne suffirait pas à pouvoir un des faubourgs de leur capitale.

vations to the same effect, that Mr. Say was fully
aware of the fact, that products of any kind may be
realised by means of commerce in the form of
provisions, at the place where they are created,
whenever provisions are more wanted at that
place than the products, whatever they may be,
in their original shape ; but that he had not sufficiently examined the system of Malthus, to perceive, what is however obvious enough and is fully
proved in the following work—that this single fact
furnishes a complete refutation of it.

The principles professed by Mr. Say on the
subject of population, are also, as it seems to me
at variance with his favorite doctrine, that there
can be no permanent excess of production in any
department of industry or in all taken together ;
but that an increase of production in any one
department, naturally gives rise to a corresponding
increase in all others, which creates in its turn an
equal augmentation in the whole amount of consumption. This principle has been contested by
Mr. Malthus, and successfully defended by Mr.
Say in several printed letters, addressed to that
gentleman ; but neither of them seem to have
perceived that it was fatal, if true, to the theory
on the subject of population professed by both.

That it is so, is however sufficiently obvious. An increase of production must be owing either to an increase in the productiveness of labor, that is to improved machinery and skill, or to an augmentation of the quantity of labor itself, that is to an increase of population. In both cases the principle of Mr. Say is equally applicable ; and it shews satisfactorily in the latter, that no inconvenience can arise from the want of provisions on account of an increase in the number of laborers, that is, of population, as long as they are all willing to work. If it is not convenient nor agreeable to them to raise their own provisions, they can employ their industry in producing any other article, in any quantity ; and such production, on the principles of Mr. Say, can never be excessive, or in other words, will always command a corresponding production and supply of any other article that may be wanted by the first producer ; and of course of the means of subsistence, until the want of these is supplied. I cannot but think that a farther consideration of the subject under this point of view, will induce Mr. Say to alter his notions upon this interesting question, and to remove in consequence one of the very few imperfections, which can justly be imputed to his valuable treatise.

Mr. de Sismondi, the distinguished author of
the Italian Republics and of many other highly
esteemed productions, has devoted to this question
several chapters of his ' New Principles of Political
Economy,'* and has approached a good deal nearer
to the truth than Mr. Say, although he has not
succeeded in freeing himself entirely from the influence of the prevailing errors.   He has perceived
and pointed out very distinctly one of the faults
in the comparison of ratios which forms the basis
of the system of Malthus ; ' This argument which
forms the basis of the system of Mr. Malthus,' says
he, ' and to which he constantly appeals throughout
his book, is completely sophistical.   It compares
the possible increase of the human race taken in the
abstract and without regard to circumstances, with
the actual increase of animals and plants on a
limited territory and in a situation constantly more
and more unfavorable.'†   This objection appears
to be perfectly just, and quite decisive.   I have also

---

* Nouveaux Principes d'Economie Politique.

† Le raisonnement, says he, Lib. 7. C. 3 qui sert de base au systême
de M. Malthus et auquel il appelle sans cesse dans tout son livre est
completement sophistique.   Il met en opposition l' accroissement possible
de la population humaine, abstraitement parlant et sans avoir egard aux
circonstances, avec l'accroissement positif des animaux et des vegetaux,
dans un lieu confine, et avec des circonstances toujours plus défa-
vorables.

urged it in the fourth and fifth chapters of the following essay ; and as I have not given credit for it to Mr. de Sismondi, it may be proper to add here, that I had not read his work at the time of composing mine. The other objection, which I have also made to the reasoning of Malthus, and which is alluded to above, to wit—that it supposes that the inhabitants of any given part of the globe must of necessity perish, unless they can find subsistence out of the products of the very soil they occupy, is also indicated by Mr. de Sismondi, although he does not appear to have felt its full importance. ‘ Mr. Malthus,’ he observes ‘ assumes as a principle that population is limited in every country by the quantity of the means of subsistence which the soil will furnish. This proposition is true, only when applied to the whole earth, or to a country which has no means of obtaining supplies from abroad. As respects all other, it is modified by the effects of foreign trade.’* Mr. Malthus supposes, without proving, the principle in question.

* M. Malthus a etabli comme principe, que la population de tout pays etait limitée par la quantité de subsistance que ce pays pouvait fournir. Cette proposition n’est vraie, qu’en l’appliquant au globe terrestre tout entier, ou à un pays qui n’a aucune possibilité de tirer des autres aucune partie de sa subsistance ; partout ailleurs le commerce etranger la modifie.

I have shewn already that a consideration of the effect of commerce not only modifies it, but refutes it altogether. But as Mr. de Sismondi does not admit the theory of Mr. Say on the subject of production, it is the less singular that he should not have perceived the full extent of the error of Malthus in this particular. Nevertheless he decidedly denies, and satisfactorily refutes the truth of the principles advanced by that writer, and has thus far rendered an important service to the cause of science.

It is remarkable, however, that Mr. de Sismondi, although he disputes the principles of Malthus which alone lend some appearance of probability to his practical conclusions, seems nevertheless to acquiesce in these conclusions, in themselves certainly not very attractive, nor very consonant with common opinion. He has the same panic terror of the excessive increase of population, the same jealousy of the operation of charity, public and private, and the same anxiety to discourage matrimony among the poor and middling classes. On this latter head he has some recommendations which I shall not venture to quote, and which whatever may be thought of their practical efficacy, shew by their singularity, the extent of his apprehensions.

Again, he remarks that, 'Public charities may be considered as encouragements held out by society, to the existence of a population which it has no means of supporting.'* He also affirms, that political institutions err much more frequently by encouraging than by preventing the increase of population ; and that Europe is now suffering from an excess in the number of its inhabitants. 'We are suffering in almost every part of Europe the calamity of an excessive population, which we have no means of supporting. For this calamity we are indebted to the imprudent zeal of our governments. With us religious instruction, legislation, the organisation of society, all combine to produce an increase of population, for the maintenance of which no means had previously been provided.'†

Any assertion or opinion, proceeding from so eminent a writer as Mr. de Sismondi, is no doubt

* La charité publique peut enfin être considerée comme un encouragement que la societé donne à une population qu'elle ne peut pas maintenir.

† Nous éprouvons aujourd'hui dans presque toute l'Europe la calamté de ne pouvoir maintenir une population surabondante. C'est à nos gouvernmens, c'est à leur zele imprudent que nous devons cette calamité. Chez nous l'instruction religieuse, la legislation, l'organisation sociale, tout a tendu à faire naitre une population à l'existence de laquelle on n'avait pas pourvu d'avance.

entitled to respect; but I confess that the above remarks appear to me very singular. Taking a survey of the surface of Europe, from the North Cape to the Straits of Gibraltar and from the coast of Portugal to the Ural Mountains, we find but two or three small spots, such as England, Holland, and Switzerland, that can be fairly considered as populous; and these are precisely the most flourishing and prosperous parts of the whole region. All the rest of Europe suffers from a want of inhabitants; and this deficiency can be traced to no other cause than vicious political institutions; which, therefore, contrary to the opinion of Mr. de Sismondi, produce an injurious effect upon society by preventing population, and not by increasing it. Are Spain, Portugal, and the south of Italy too populous? Is there an excess of inhabitants in Poland, Austria, Hungary, Russia, and Turkey? France itself, one of the most flourishing States in Europe, might maintain a hundred and fifty millions of inhabitants as well as thirty. Ireland alone is often cited as an example of a country that suffers from excessive population; but Ireland is not more populous than England, Holland, Switzerland, and some of the northern parts of Italy. If it be less prosperous, the cause must be looked for in some other circumstance.

As to the encouragement given to population by direct inducements to marriage held out by the magistrates or clergy, of which Mr. de Sismondi is so much afraid, it is evident that they are entirely nugatory, and can do in general neither good nor harm. The natural inducements to form this connexion are too strong, to require or admit of any reinforcement from the effect of religious or political considerations; and a law for the encouragement of marriage is very much like one for encouraging the sun to rise in the morning, or the rivers to run down hill. As a general proposition the whole population of every country must, will, and do marry. Where there is a deficiency of inhabitants, it is not because there are not marriages enough, but because the children die in infancy from the wretchedness and poverty of their parents. Where there is an excess of population, (which can never be any other than a temporary condition,) it is not because there are too many marriages, but because the vicious organisation of the society does not permit the people to work, or to enjoy the fruits of their labor. Marriage instead of requiring to be encouraged, is itself the great encouragement to labor, and the great relief and solace under hardships and privations. It was

so regarded among the venerable fathers of our
race.   What was the prize for which the Patriarch
labored seven years in succession, and then seven
years more at the end of them ?   Was it not the
hand of Rachel, that was held out to him as the
reward of his tedious toils, and was it not reward
enough ?   Did not the love that he bore her make
his fourteen long years appear to him but as one
day ?   Did he wait for a legislative act to encourage him to marry her at the end of that time ?
The object of the magistrate in holding out inducements to marriage, is to persuade Jacob to espouse
Rachel—as if he were not ready enough to do it
before.   Let the government take care not to play
the part of Laban, and the Jacobs and Rachels
will soon find their way to each other's arms.   Mr.
de Sismondi who is so much alarmed at the danger
of these legislative inducements, may, I believe, set
his heart at rest.   If there be really any reasonable
ground to fear an excess of marriages, he must
look for the cause in the enactments of a higher
authority than that of any of our magistrates.

The paradoxical and unsocial principles to which
I have here alluded were first broached by Mr.
Malthus, as necessary though not agreeable conclu-
sions from his system ; and they fall to the ground

of themselves when the theory that supported them is found to fail. It is singular, therefore, that Mr. de Sismondi, who denies the theory, should yet receive the conclusions ; and lend the high authority of his name in giving them additional currency.

In the following work, I have not only endeavored to refute the system of Malthus, but also to establish the new, or rather to restore the old principle that the increase of population, is in fact, the immediate moving cause of public prosperity. Should this principle be satisfactorily made out, it will form, I think, an important addition to the science of political economy as it now stands. The progress of society in civilisation has been traced immediately by Adam Smith to the division of labor ; and in this hypothesis he has been followed by most subsequent writers. But what is the origin of that division ? The answer of Smith to this question is to my mind by no means satisfactory. He traces it to an innate and instinctive disposition in the human race to 'truck, barter and exchange.' That there is any such innate disposition is perhaps very doubtful ; and if there be, it can hardly be supposed powerful enough to serve as the main spring of the whole machinery of society. In the following work, I have traced the origin of the division of labor to the increase of population ; and thus carried it back to the strongest of our natural instincts. For the developement and proof of the principle, I must refer the reader to the work itself.

Since the first publication of this essay, I have had opportunity to examine the treatise of Mr. Gray, entitled *The Happiness of States*, which I had not then seen. He coincides with me in asserting the favorable effect of the increase of population and in contesting the theory of Malthus, but has not advanced the same arguments with mine either in favor of our common principle, or in opposition to our common antagonist ; so that the two works have very little resemblance, excepting in their general tendency. Mr. Gray is, I think, rather wanting in precision, and too much inclined to coin new words ; but his work is remarkable for the excellent spirit that pervades the whole of it, for the general justness of the reasoning, and for the large and valuable collection of facts by which the theory is illustrated ; so that it forms an important addition to the literature of political economy. It has been abridged and presented in a form rather more popular than the original one by Dr. Purves.

Madrid, November 1, 1825.

PREFACE

TO THE FIRST EDITION.

———◆———

The following tract was prepared for publication upon the Continent during the last winter.* A reperusal of the Essay of Mr. Malthus on Population, and some conversations which I held at the time with a friend upon the subject of it, suggested to me certain views which I thought new, and which are quite at variance with the conclusions of that eminent philosopher. Without feeling any extraordinary confidence in my own ideas—especially where they differ from those of an author of great and just celebrity, whose theories have been sanctioned by the favorable opinion of many competent judges—I have nevertheless concluded to submit these views to the Public. I shall certainly be

*1822.

highly gratified if they are found to throw any new
light upon the interesting question to which they
relate, not only because it is always agreeable and
honorable to aid in the discovery of truth, but
because the views which I have taken appear to
me to be in themselves more consonant to the best
affections of our nature, than the system which is
now so generally received.   I should not certainly
go the length of saying—as Cicero did of Epicurus
and Plato—that I would rather be in the wrong
upon my own principles than in the right upon
those of Mr. Malthus ;—but I have no hesitation
in admitting, that it would give me pain, independently of any personal considerations, to be convinced of the error of my opinions, and of the
truth of a theory which tends so strongly as his to
embitter the ' cordial drop of life.'   However the
Public may decide upon the substance of this little
tract, I venture to hope that it will be recognised,
in its form and spirit, as the production of a friend
of truth and human happiness.   In digesting the
materials, I have principally aimed at brevity :
and shall be quite satisfied, if it shall be found that
the higher and more essential merit of perspicuity
has been no where sacrificed to this consideration.

Upon my arrival in town a few weeks since for the purpose of superintending the impression of the work, I took an opportunity of mentioning the subject to my illustrious friend Sir James Mackintosh, and of explaining to him the general scope of the argument. This great statesman and philosopher—whose name I feel it a high honor to be able to mention in connexion with my own—upon learning that the Essay which I had prepared was intended in part to correct the theory of Mr. Malthus, kindly invited me to go down with him to the East India College, and converse with that gentleman upon the subject. I accepted this proposal with much pleasure, as well from a natural desire to make the acquaintance of so eminent a writer, as from the reflection, that if I had accidentally taken up any misconception of his views, I should probably be able to rectify it by a free communication with him upon the points in controversy. Had I found this to be the case, I was fully prepared to sacrifice my own ideas and suppress the work.

I had always been highly gratified with the candid and temperate tone that distinguishes the writings of Mr. Malthus, although I have not been so fortunate as to agree with him in his leading principles,—and I hope that I shall not be thought to pass the bounds of delicacy in adding, that I found his conversation the perfect counterpart, in this respect, of his works. I have rarely met with a finer specimen of the true philosophic temper, graced and set off by the urbanity of a finished gentleman, than is seen in his person. I feel myself greatly indebted to him for the very hospitable reception which he was pleased to give me ; and for the kindness and courtesy with which he entered into all the explanations that I requested in regard to his opinions. I should pay him a very poor compliment, if I were to suppose it possible that he could be offended by a free expression of opinions different from his own : and I trust that there is nothing in the tone and manner of the following tract, that will tend in the slightest degree to wound his feelings. If, however, I should have been led unconsciously, by the warmth of composition and argument, to make use of any language that would naturally produce this effect, I beg leave here to disavow most explicitly any such intention, and to assure Mr. Malthus of the high respect and esteem that I feel for his character. Such indeed is my estimation of the

intellectual and moral qualities of this gentleman, that I believe he would not only adopt
without reluctance a different opinion from that
which he has hitherto held, if he were satisfied
of its truth ; but that he would do this with real
pleasure, if the new opinion were in its nature
more agreeable and social than the other.

It would be an unbecoming violation of the
confidence of private intercourse to detail particularly the conversations which I held with Mr.
Malthus upon the subject of the Essay ; and it
would also be useless for the present purpose, as
very little, if any thing, was said on his part, that
is not contained in his printed works, or on mine,
that will not be found in the following tract.
After a full and free discussion of all the points
in dispute, I was satisfied that the difference of
opinion between us did not arise from any mis-
understanding on either side, but from a difference in our modes of considering the subject,
resulting perhaps originally from accident, but
confirmed by habit, and not to be affected by a
few conversations.   I had therefore no reason to
change my intention of publishing the present
work.

It was suggested to me by Mr. Malthus, that the leading principle maintained in it, is the same in substance with that of a work on Population by Mr. S. Gray. I have never read the work of Mr. Gray, and have not had an opportunity of consulting it since, for the purpose of comparing his ideas with mine. Should they be in fact the same, my views, though original, would not be entitled to the name which I have given them of *New Ideas.* Even in this case, however, as the work of Mr. Gray does not seem to have made much impression upon public opinion, a republication of the same views, by a different hand, and in a new form, might not be without its use. But I am inclined to think, from a hasty reference to some passages of his book at the house of Mr. Malthus, and from the observations of that gentleman upon his principles, that he has not anticipated the theory of the present essay in its most essential points.

London, May 20, 1823.

New Ideas on Population.

CHAPTER I.

Introductory Remarks.

THE origin of moral and physical evil is a problem that attracted the attention of reflecting minds at a very early period, but has not yet been brought to a satisfactory solution. The most ancient literary memorials now extant prove that this subject was examined with a high degree of interest in the very infancy of society; and the inquiry has been pursued ever since without intermission, although with different degrees of zeal and industry, up to the present day.

Among the various theories that have been suggested for the solution of this question, is the one which was extensively propagated and received about the close of the last century, and which refers the origin of evil to the vices of political institutions, or, as stated in its most exaggerated form, to the mere fact of their existence. It supposes that man, in his natural state, was wise, virtuous, healthy, and happy; but that he had been depraved and rendered miserable by the effect of social union. These premises being admitted, it follows of course that the abolition of political institutions would remove the principle of evil, and restore the human race to its primitive state of perfect innocence and happiness. It is even maintained by the Marquis de Condorcet, one of the most distinguished French writers who adopted these views, that under the circumstances supposed, death itself would disappear, and that men would become immortal upon the face of the earth. Mr. Godwin, in his Political Justice, does not, if I rightly remember, directly encourage this last opinion; but holds in every other respect the same system, and conceives that the destruction of government, religion, property, and marriage, with the subsidiary institutions of less importance that make up the fabric of society, would effect at once a return of the golden age.

This theory, thus pursued into its necessary consequences, is sufficiently alarming; but,

when coolly considered, presents no great difficulty to an opponent. In the extravagant form
in which it was produced by Condorcet, it is of
course unworthy of attention, and refutes itself
at once. In reply to its more reasonable advocates, it may be remarked that the principle of
evil is evidently an original ingredient in the
system of the universe; and that if man had
been constituted by nature for a life of perfect
innocence and happiness, he could not possibly
have made himself miserable and vicious, either
by means of social institutions, or in any other
way; that the theory in question is directly con-
tradicted by the whole experience of the world,
which shows that man is indebted to political
institutions, taken in the large sense in which
the phrase is here used, for almost all the virtue
and happiness which he ever attains, and that
his situation is uniformly more favorable, in proportion as these institutions obtain a greater degree of consolidation and efficacy. To these
considerations it may be added, that the expectation of deriving happiness from individual independence is entirely inconsistent with the principles of our nature, which compel us, on the
contrary, to seek for it exclusively in the society

of each other, and in various relations, all of which imply a mutual dependence to a greater or less degree.

These ideas would probably be decisive with reflecting minds. There is however a further objection to the theory of Mr. Godwin, which presents itself in a still more positive and material shape. As moral and physical evil, in the various forms in which they operate, furnish the only checks to the increase of population which we can perceive or imagine, it follows of course, that if these checks should cease to operate by the removal of their causes, population would proceed with great rapidity, until at no very distant period the whole earth would be overstocked with inhabitants, and physical and moral evil would reappear in the form of famine, and its necessary effects. This argument is therefore a complete *reductio ad absurdum* of the doctrine of perfectibility for all who have not the courage to deny, with Mr. Godwin, that the human race has any power of increase at all. The objection, though obvious, does not appear to have attracted the public attention until it was for the first time distinctly and powerfully stated by Mr. Malthus in the Essay on Population.   If

this writer had confined himself to a simple developement of this proposition, he might have
claimed perhaps the credit of a discovery in
political science ; and his work would have certainly been valuable, though not quite so important as it has sometimes been considered.

But as the theory which Mr. Malthus under-
took to refute was in a great measure the result
of the political enthusiasm of the time, so the
character of his refutation appears to have been
determined or modified by a reaction of this
enthusiasm. The advocates of the system of
perfectibility were anxious to reduce their ideas
to practice by abolishing, or at least considerably
altering, the existing institutions of the countries
to which they belonged : or rather their pre-
tended system was only a generalisation, in an
exaggerated form, of their views in regard to
immediate political objects. Hence the first
point with their opponents was to prove the
inexpediency of actual reform, rather than to
attack the abstract theories of the reformers ;
and any argument which served the latter of
these purposes, without at the same time securing
the other was, for the moment, irrelevant and
useless. Now the general considerations, which

I have stated as furnishing a sufficient answer to
the abstract doctrine of perfectibility, were en-
cumbered with this difficulty.   They all suppose
the value of political institutions ; and hence,
instead of discouraging, rather favor any rational
attempt to improve them ; since a thing which
is good in itself will probably be the better the
nearer it is brought to the perfection of which
its nature is capable.   In like manner the argument, derived from the increase of population,
though decisive against the possibility of a state
of perfect innocence and happiness, does not
touch, in the slightest degree, the question of
political improvement.   It was natural enough,
therefore, that Mr. Malthus, not finding this
argument sufficient for his purpose in its obvious
and true shape, should have been led to modify
it, and to present it in a form in which it would
be more immediately useful.

In order to refute the abstract system of perfectibility, and at the same time to demonstrate
the inexpediency of reforming existing institutions, Mr. Malthus passes over somewhat lightly
the argument, that if we suppose the non-existence of evil, the world would soon be overstocked with inhabitants, and that famine with its

attendant miseries would speedily follow. This result, he remarks, is too remote to be a proper theme for speculation. He presents the argument in a different shape, or rather he advances an entirely new one, and maintains that in consequence of the laws of nature, which regulate the increase of the human species, and of the means of their subsistence, there does actually, and must of necessity, exist in all ages and countries, and in all the stages of civilisation, a disproportion between the demand for food and its supply; or in other words, that there is now, always has been, and always will be, throughout the whole world, a perpetual famine. This famine is the ultimate cause of all our sufferings; or in other words, is the origin of evil. As it is a necessary consequence of the standing laws of nature, the existence of evil is also necessary; and as it has no connexion with political institutions, the greater or less degree of perfection to which these institutions may be brought can have no effect upon it. Hence it would be idle on this supposition to expect relief for any sufferings to which society may be exposed in political reform ; and the argument, if well grounded is, for the immediate purpose of Mr. Malthus, conclusive. Considered as an answer to Godwin, it is somewhat similar to the process which is called at law proving an *alibi*. In order to show that the evil we suffer does not proceed from political institutions, Mr. Malthus points out another cause, from which he affirms that it does proceed. His work has therefore, as well as that of Mr. Godwin, the merit of furnishing a new theory on the long-contested question of the origin of evil.

The attempt to prove an *alibi* is generally considered at law as somewhat dangerous; since this sort of defence, however triumphant, if completely successful, amounts to an abandonment of every other; and, if not made out, is therefore a surrender of the case. In philosophy, the danger is not perhaps in general so great. It may be remarked, however, that in this particular case Mr. Malthus, by insisting on the argument alluded to, loses the advantage of most of the objections that may really be urged against the system of Godwin, and which have been recapitulated in a preceding page; since they all suppose the value of political institutions, which is denied by implication in the doctrine of Malthus. It is in fact somewhat singular, that while the immediate object of Godwin was to demonstrate the expediency of practical reform, and that of Malthus to prove its inutility, the theories of both these writers admit on general grounds of precisely the same answer. While Godwin considers political institutions as absolutely mischievous, Malthus affirms that they are completely indifferent. The true answer to both is, that they are neither mischievous nor indifferent, but extremely valuable : that the origin of evil is not to be found in the existence of society, nor in any supposed law of nature which creates a necessity of perpetual famine, but in the primary constitution of the universe : that the world was not intended for a Paradise, nor man for a state of perfect innocence and bliss ; but that we are principally indebted to the influence of society for the measure of happiness which we are able to obtain and fitted to enjoy.

If the value of social institutions be admitted, it follows of necessity that the theory of Mr Malthus, which supposes their indifference must be false, and the reasoning by which it is supported without sufficient foundation. But however conclusive this general answer to his system may justly be considered, it is still by no means

a superfluous task to examine in detail the arguments which he has brought in proof of it.   His
work is entitled to great attention, as well from
the ability displayed in it, as from the approbation that has been bestowed upon it in the most
respectable quarters.   His reasoning is also of
such a kind, that if well established, it super-
sedes any other arguments of a different description.   Moral evidence, however strong, must
give way to mathematical demonstration : and
we must admit, if necessary, with Mr. Malthus,
that social institutions are matters of indifference,
or even with Mr. Godwin, that they are the
sources of all evil, rather than deny that two
and two make four.

CHAPTER II.

On the Economical Effect of an Increase of Population.

THE economical effect of an increase of population, is an augmentation in the supply of labor and in the demand for its products. The wants of the new comers create the new demand, and their labor furnishes the new supply. These principles are too obvious to require any development; yet Mr. Malthus seems either to have not perceived them, or not to have kept them distinctly in view. He appears throughout his work to consider the increase of population, simply in its effect upon the consumption of the means of subsistence, without regarding its operation upon their supply. He views every individual added to a society as an additional consumer, without appearing to reflect, that he is also at the same time an additional laborer. This consideration alone, if properly estimated, is sufficient, I think, to rectify the whole theory of this writer, and to refute its paradoxical and dangerous parts. I propose in this and the next chapter to develope the principle above stated, and to consider its application to the condition of society in the various stages of civilisation.

As the effect of an increase of population is an augmentation in the supply of labor, and an increased demand for its products, the question naturally arises in what manner the proportion previously existing between the demand for these products and their supply is affected by this cause. Does an increase of population produce an increased supply of the products of labor in proportion to the demand, and consequently a greater abundance of the necessaries and comforts of life ; or does it, on the contrary, produce an increased demand for the products of labor in proportion to the supply, and consequently a comparative distress and scarcity ? This is the real question upon which the whole inquiry turns, and is the one which Mr. Malthus has attempted to bring to a summary decision, by a sort of mathematical demonstration. I shall consider hereafter the value of this argument in a separate chapter, and shall only observe at present, that Mr. Malthus has been led by it to adopt the affirmative of the latter of the above questions, and to maintain, as was intimated in the last chapter, that the increase of population necessarily produces distress and scarcity. It appears to me, on the contrary, that the affirmative of the former question is true, and that the effect of an increase of population is to produce a comparative abundance of all the articles of enjoyment and use; as I shall endeavor to show by considerations drawn immediately from observation and experience.

If we regard the labor of an individual and its products as fixed quantities; that is, if we suppose one man to labor naturally as much as another, and that a given amount of labor will always produce an equal quantity of useful objects; it is evident that an increase of population can have no tendency to occasion either a scarcity or an abundance of the means of subsistence. The additional supply created by such an increase would correspond exactly with the additional demand resulting from the same cause, and the proportion between them would remain the same as before. This supposition, however, is far from being correct. The labor of individuals and the amount of its products, both vary under different circumstances; and it is therefore necessary for the solution of the present question, to consider what these circumstances are, and how they are affected by an increase of population.

1. The labor of individuals is by no means a fixed quantity, but varies with their natural dispositions, and with the motives that determine their conduct. We observe a remarkable difference in the activity and industry of different communities, and of different persons in the same community, resulting from varieties of situation and character. For the present purpose, however, the labor of individuals may be taken as uniform; since it is obvious that the distress, which may result from a mere indisposition to labor, can have no connexion with any general law of nature regulating the proportion between the demand for the means of subsistence and their supply.

2. The circumstances that determine the productiveness of labor are necessarily two, the natural advantages under which it is applied, and the skill employed in its application. The same quantity of labor will produce a hundred bushels of corn in Mexico, and only ten in Norway: nor could any effort of industry obtain the

delicious wines of France and Italy from the
soil of Great Britain. The effect of a difference
in skill is equally remarkable. A single miller
will grind more corn in a day than twenty men
would be able to pound up into powder by hand :
and a single weaver will weave more cloth in an
equal time, than a dozen persons who labor without a machine. These illustrations obviously
afford a very moderate representation of the differences in the productiveness of labor resulting
from the varieties of natural advantages, and of
skill under which it is directed. For the present
purpose the advantages of nature, as well as the
labor of individuals, may be considered as uniform ; since the increase of population can have
no immediate effect in altering the soil, climate,
or other natural properties of the country in which
it occurs. Of the several causes that determine
the amount of the means of subsistence which
will be obtained by the labor of a given number
of individuals, the only one therefore which must
be regarded as variable for the purpose of this
inquiry, is the skill with which their labor is applied. Hence the question, whether an increase
of population tends to produce an abundance or
a scarcity of the means of subsistence, resolves

itself into the further one, whether such increase produces a favorable or an unfavorable effect upon the skill employed in the application of labor.

The question being thus reduced to its proper terms, few intelligent persons, I apprehend, will hesitate much about the manner in which it should be answered. It is sufficiently notorious, that an increase of population on a given territory is followed immediately by a division of labor ; which produces in its turn the invention of new machines, an improvement of methods in all the departments of industry, and a rapid progress in the various branches of art and science. The increase effected by these improvements in the productiveness of labor is obviously much greater in proportion than the increase of population, to which it is owing. The population of Great Britain, for example, doubled itself in the course of the last century, while the improvements in the modes of applying labor, made during the same period, have increased its productiveness so much, that it would probably be a moderate estimate to consider its products as a thousand times greater than before. If, however, we suppose the increase in the products of labor, naturally resulting from the doubling of a population on a given territory, to be only in the proportion of ten to one, the means of subsistence will still be more abundant in the proportion of five to one, than they were before. And on this very low calculation, the respective rates of increase in the amount of population, and the means of subsistence, comparatively stated, will be as follows: to wit, for the population, 1. 2. 4. 8. 16, &c. and for the means of subsistence, 1. 10. 100. 1000, &c.

This statement of ratios is more comfortable, and, I believe, far more correct, than that of Mr. Malthus. But this estimate, though moderate, is still much higher than it need be, in order to refute the system of this writer. It is only necessary for this purpose to suppose, that the increase in the products of labor exactly keeps pace with the increase of population; as, for example, that the additional supply of laborers, together with the improvement of methods and invention of machines, resulting from the doubling of a population on a given territory, only maintains the productiveness of labor at the same point at which it stood before, and consequently doubles its products. Even upon this estimate, however much below the truth, the supply of the means of subsistence remains the same, notwithstanding the increase of consumers. In order to substantiate the theory of Malthus, it is necessary to adopt the strange supposition, that labor becomes less efficient and productive in proportion to the degree of skill with which it is applied; that a man can raise more weight by hand, than by the help of a lever, and see further with the naked eye than with the best telescope. These positions are not, it is true, directly taken by this writer, but they are necessarily implied in the general propositions which he has attempted to establish.

I have considered it safe, to take for granted, that an increase of population on a given territory necessarily and naturally produces a division of labor, and a consequent increase of skill in its application. No intelligent person would probably undertake to dispute this principle; but as it forms the basis of the argument contained in the present essay, it may be proper to develope it a little more fully, by taking a rapid view of the effect of the increase of population, as it operates at different stages in the progress of society. This exposition will form the subject of the following chapter.

CHAPTER III.

On the Economical Effect of an Increase of Population at Different Stages in the Progress of Society.

It is somewhere observed by Rousseau that he had passed his life in reading voyages and travels. This fact does not tend, I think, to diminish the surprise, which judicious and reflecting men have generally felt at finding so powerful a writer maintain that man is by nature an isolated and independent being, and that his situation is more eligible in this his natural condition, than it is in the artificial and unnatural one of society. The position that individual independence is the natural state of man, and society an unnatural institution, is plainly the direct reverse of the truth. But independently of this objection, it seems almost incredible that any observer of tolerable discretion, and especially one so intelligent and highly gifted as Rousseau, should retain a favorable opinion of the savage state, after reading habitually the accounts that are given by travellers of the tribes and nations which they have found in a condition approaching in any degree to that of individual independence. It is a painful consideration, that the human race is capable, under any circumstances, of sinking into the state of moral degradation which these uncivilised communities almost uniformly exhibit: and it would be a melancholy thing indeed to suppose that man was formed and intended by nature for this degraded condition; and of course that he has a constant tendency to return to it, whenever he has been forced unnaturally into a state of civilisation. Such opinions are happily as false as they are unpleasant. We know, by observing the principles of our nature, that we were intended for society: and we find accordingly, that it is only in the bosom of society and civilisation, that the human character unfolds itself in its real elevation and beauty. It is there only that man displays the talents, virtues, and graces, that adorn and dignify his nature, and reaps the highest enjoyments of which he is capable. A state of individual independence, or one in any degree approaching to it, is therefore not the state of nature, but a savage state; that is, an unnatural and degraded condition, into which certain fractions of the human family are thrown by misfortune or accident; where they are unable to follow out the instinct of nature and the dictates of reason, which both lead to the establishment of social institutions ; and where they can neither attain the accomplishments nor enjoy the pleasures, which in other circumstances would have been within their reach. The North American Indians furnish one of the most favorable specimens that have yet been found of men in the savage state : and they appear to be the wrecks of more flourishing and populous communities, in which the principle of prosperity must have been destroyed by the operation of some unfavorable cause.

In such a state of society it is difficult to suppose the possibility of an increase of population. The quantity of labor employed for the purpose of obtaining the means of subsistence is immense ; while the fruits afforded by it are scanty and wretched. This single object employs the whole time and attention of the savage ; and even the wars in which he is perpetually engaged are generally connected with it. Still the supply of the necessaries and comforts of life is so inadequate to his wants, and the hardships to which he is exposed so oppressive, that human nature sinks under the burden of them : and the population is in most cases found to be in a state of gradual diminution. If however we suppose an increase of population to be effected by the operation of some accidental cause, it is evident that the consequence will be an immediate improvement in the condition of the society. If the tribe be in the hunter state there will now be two hunters where there was before only one, or three where there were only two. They will go out in larger companies, and employ better instruments and more ingenious stratagems. In this way the quantity of game will be increased in a proportion much larger than that of the increase in the number of the hunters. Thus life will become easier, and the supply of necessaries and comforts more abundant, supposing even that the principal employment of the society remains the same as before.

The ultimate effect of an increase of population in such a community, if continued for any length of time, would however probably be to effect a transition to an easier and more civilized mode of living, and to introduce the adoption of agriculture as the principal means of obtaining subsistence.

Agriculture, as it is the most agreeable and productive of all occupations, and the only one that admits of any considerable progress in population and civilisation, may well be considered as the natural employment of man. The few scanty and barbarous tribes that live by the rude resources of hunting and fishing, and even those in the shepherd state, as the Laplanders, the Tartars, and the Bedouin Arabs, may therefore be looked upon, as I just now remarked, not as specimens of men in a state of nature, but of men who have sunk by misfortune or accident below the state of nature, and who will probably never be able to return to it, unless they should be led by some other accident of a more favorable kind to resort to the cultivation of the soil. The adoption of agriculture as the principal means of obtaining subsistence is followed immediately and necessarily by the introduction of commerce and manufactures. While the hunter can hardly obtain by incessant toil and exposure to intolerable hardships, a wretched and scanty supply of the articles of first necessity, the husbandman procures by easy and mo-

derate labor an ample provision for himself and
several other persons.   This abundance of the
first and most necessary articles naturally introduces the desire for comforts and pleasures of a
higher character.   The superfluous portion of
the products is converted into new and more
agreeable forms; and the success of the first
attempts made for this purpose is followed by
a continual course of improvements upon the
same plan.   Such is the origin of manufactures:
and these in their turn suppose and require the
existence of commerce.   While a part of the
community is exclusively employed in obtaining
by the cultivation of the soil, the natural products
required for the use of the whole, another portion
would in like manner be exclusively employed in
giving new forms to the superfluous portion of
these products: and these two divisions of society would exchange with each other the fruits of
their respective labors.   Such is the origin of
commerce, which naturally becomes, like agriculture and manufactures, the exclusive employment
of a part of the community.   These three occupations therefore, each of which supposes and
requires the existence of the others, and of
which agriculture is the principal, form together
the natural employments of the human race.

We find, accordingly, that these employments have been almost universally adopted throughout the world, at all the periods of history of which we have any knowledge. Of the seven or eight hundred millions at which the population of the globe has been loosely calculated, probably not more than five or six millions have ever in any age subsisted by the ruder arts of the hunter, the fisherman, or the herdsman : and this scanty and wretched fragment of the species might, perhaps, be looked upon as an intermediate link in the chain of being between men and the other animals with more propriety than as a genuine portion of the human race. Yet by a strange sort of caprice it is precisely among these degraded and barbarous clans that the poets of every age have delighted to lay the scenes of their pictures of tenderness and heroism : and by an aberration still stranger, if possible, the philosophers of every age have exhibited an almost uniform disposition to treat these bastard scions of the human stock as the true specimens of its ordinary growth, and to consider all variations from them as alterations of the natural standard, by improvement according to some, and by corruption according to others. This error is like that of a botanist, who should estimate the size of the great magnolia tree by the height that it reaches in the latitude of Boston : and should consider the colossal stature and glorious display of flowers and foliage with which nature adorns this splendid plant in the climate of Florida as artificial and monstrous. The natural situation of every animal or plant is plainly the one in which it thrives best with the least forcing.

Agriculture, therefore, with its attendant occupations, manufactures and commerce, being the natural and almost universal employment of man, the question as to the effect of the increase of population upon the supply of the means of subsistence, is principally important as applied to a society in this condition. What then is the effect of an increase of population upon such a society? It is evidently an extension of the power of the society in all its branches, intellectual and physical, and in all the modes in which this power is applied, according to the degree in which they are severally encouraged by this influence of political and physical causes. Additional tracts of land will be brought under cultivation. The conversion to new uses of the surplus products which they afford beyond the demand for immediate consumption, will open a new field for manufacturing and commercial industry : and labor in all its branches being now pursued upon a larger scale, its division will be more complete, and the consequent increase of productiveness and improvement of methods will be more remarkable. If the country is so situated in itself, and in relation to others, as to hold out great inducements to the occupation of new tracts of land, and the exchange of their surplus products for the manufactures of other nations, the increase of population will stimulate agricultural and commercial more than manufacturing industry, as in the United States of America. If, as in England, the occupation of new tracts of land to any considerable extent is impossible, while the situation of the country and the nature of its foreign relations hold out great encouragement to manufactures and commerce ; it is in the rapid extension of these forms of labor, that the effect of the increase of population will be principally observable. In either case, and in all cases, it will be found the fruitful source of national wealth and abundance. The increase of population is to nature, what

the natural growth of the body is to individuals.
As long as an individual continues to grow, he
obtains continually new accessions of intellectual and physical power, either by the acquisition
of new faculties, or by a more complete developement of those which he possessed before :
and thus a nation, where the population is
increasing, is constantly augmenting its resources
and its power, without being compelled, like
individuals, to look forward to a definite period,
when this state of progression must cease, and
give way to a contrary course of decay and final
dissolution.

The amount of labor at the disposal of the
society, and the skill with which it is applied,
being thus augmented, in proportion to the
increase of population, it is evident that the
result must be a great increase of products. The
greater or less degree of abundance, as respects
the means of subsistence, which will result from
this increase, will depend upon the physical and
political situation of the society, and the greater
or less degree in which the several departments
of industry are favored by it. It seems to be
the opinion of Mr. Malthus, that as long as there
are large tracts of land in a country to be occu-

pied, the increase of population is unattended with danger; and that it is only when the soil has been entirely appropriated, while the population still continues to increase, that the danger of scarcity begins to present itself. But in this, as in many other points, the positions of Mr. Malthus seem to be directly the reverse of the truth. As long as the principal effect of the increase of population, is to bring under cultivation additional tracts of land, the positive resources and wealth of the society will doubtless be augmented in the same proportion, but the means of subsistence will be neither more nor less abundant than they were before. Let us suppose, for example, that a hundred families obtain an easy and abundant subsistence by cultivating five hundred acres of land. If the number of families be increased to two hundred, and the number of acres under cultivation to a thousand; it is obvious, that the proportion between the demand for the means of subsistence and their supply will not be altered. It is only when the population begins to increase upon a territory already appropriated, that it produces the effect of augmenting the supply of the provisions in proportion to the demand. In the

former case, the supply of labor is augmented,
but the skill with which it is applied remains
nearly the same as before. In the latter, the
skill as well as the number of the laborers is
increased ; and as the productiveness of labor
depends almost wholly upon the skill and science with which it is applied, it is obvious, that
the products will be infinitely more abundant in
the latter case, with the same increase of population, than they were in the former. The increase of population on an unoccupied territory
only increases the quantity of rude labor and of
its products, but leaves the productiveness of
labor and the comparative abundance of its products as before. On a limited territory, the
same cause introduces the new element of skill,
the effects of which, in augmenting the productiveness of labor, and the abundance of its
products, are unbounded and incalculable.

The result, in the latter case, is naturally a
great and immediate extension of manufactures
and commerce. The fine productions of skilful
labor, after satisfying the demand of the neighboring nations, are carried to the most distant
parts of the world, and bring back the coarser
natural productions to be used for consumption

or wrought up into these fine fabrics. This exchange is advantageous to both parties, and
especially to the civilised or populous community. The labor of a single member of such a
society will perhaps purchase the product of that
of a hundred barbarian hunters. A few glass
beads, which may be valued at nothing, are converted, by the help of the machinery employed
in navigation, into a princely fortune. To faci-
litate these exchanges, some of the inhabitants
of the populous nations fix themselves in foreign
countries. At first they generally return after
realising the immediate object of their expedition. But as the settlements which they make
for commercial purposes gradually become more
agreeable places of residence, many persons are
induced to remain, and establish themselves for
life. In this way emigration and colonisation
are introduced in connexion with manufactures
and commerce. In the new settlements that
are thus formed, labor is applied with skill, and
is proportionally productive : while population,
encouraged by the high state of civilisation, proceeds with rapidity. These flourishing establishments are naturally employed almost wholly
in agriculture ; and resort to the mother-country,

in order to exchange its fruits for the fine products of taste and art. Thus the rapid growth
of these young scions, instead of exhausting the
parent stock, gives it new health and vigor ; and
a dense and increasing population on a limited
territory, instead of bringing with it any danger
of scarcity, is not only an immediate cause of
greater abundance to the nation where it exists,
but a principle of prosperity and civilisation to
every part of the world. The history of most
of the populous nations with which we are acquainted confirms the truth of these remarks :
and they are illustrated in a particular manner
by that of Great Britain and the United States
of America. If well grounded, they are decisive of the whole question, in regard to the influence of the increase of population upon the
supply of the means of subsistence, and prove
conclusively that the theory of Mr. Malthus is
not only erroneous, but directly the reverse of
the truth ; and that an increase of population,
instead of being, as he maintains, the chief
cause of all the physical and moral evil to which
we are exposed, is, on the contrary, the real and
only active principle of national wealth and happiness.

To these remarks, however inconsistent with his theory, Mr. Malthus has nothing to oppose, but his well-known argument of the difference, established by a law of nature between the ratios of the increase of population and of the means of subsistence. The conclusion which he deduces from a comparison of these ratios forms the whole foundation of his system. It is therefore necessary, in order to substantiate the principles maintained in this and the preceding chapter, to examine the value of this celebrated argument. It will be found, I think, upon closer inspection, to be much less formidable, than it has generally been supposed.

CHAPTER IV.

On the Natural Proportion between the Rates of Increase of Population and of the Means of Subsistence.

As the quantity of the means of subsistence which can be obtained from a limited territory is also of necessity limited, if we suppose the number of the inhabitants of such a territory to be regularly increasing for an indefinite length of time, and if we also suppose that they are obliged to subsist upon the direct products of the soil which they occupy, it will follow of course, that there must be sooner or later an excess of population and a deficiency of food. This proposition is perfectly obvious, but of very little practical importance, excepting in its application to the abstract theory of perfectability. In the hands of Mr. Malthus, it assumes the following shape :

The human species possesses a power of increase capable of doubling the population of any given territory, as often at least as once in twenty-five years : But

The quantity of the means of subsistence, which can be obtained from a given territory, cannot be augmented to the same extent, nor faster at the utmost, than by the addition of an equal quantity, once in twenty-five years.

Hence while the population increases with the rapidity of a geometrical progression, the means of subsistence can only be augmented in the manner of an arithmetical one, and the two rates of increase compared together, will stand as follows : to wit, that of population as, 1. 2. 4. 8. 16. &c. and that of food as, 1. 2. 3. 4. 5. 6. &c.

From this comparison, Mr. Malthus concludes that in every country the population has a constant tendency to increase beyond the supply of provisions, or in his favorite phrase presses hard against it. This metaphorical language is equivalent to the plainer statement, that in every country a considerable part of the population must always of necessity be distressed for want of food. The proposition is neither very agreeable, nor very consistent with experience. It is certainly, however, a fair and necessary conclu-

sion from the above comparison of ratios : and
hence if it be erroneous, the defect in the argument must be looked for in the premises. By
comparing the statement of this argument, made
by Mr. Malthus, with the simpler one given at
the beginning of this chapter, it will be easy to
perceive the nature of the error. It will be
seen that Mr. Malthus has taken for granted the
correctness of two suppositions, neither of which
is in fact true. It is not true that the human
race possesses a rapid and indefinite power of
increase, under the checks to which the progress of population is subject ; and it is not
true that the inhabitants of a given tract of territory must necessarily subsist upon the direct
products of the soil they occupy. Thus the
premises of the argument contain two distinct
errors, either of which would alone vitiate completely the force of the conclusion.

As I propose to treat in a separate chapter
the subject of the real power of increase in the
human species, I shall omit for the present any
further notice of the first of these false suppositions, and confine myself to an exposition of
the second. The error in this is so very obvious, that it is really singular how it should have

escaped the observation of **Mr. Malthus.** It is perfectly plain that there is no necessity why the occupant or occupants of a given tract of land should subsist upon the direct products of their own soil. The proposition, if true, would hold with the same force of provinces, cities, and individuals, as of independent states ; and the error will be seen at once, by applying the argument to one of these cases in which the conclusion is notoriously false : as for example, to that of the city of London. It would then stand as follows.

The population of the city of London has the power of doubling itself every twenty-five years, or of increasing in the manner of a geometrical progression : But

The means of subsistence which can be obtained from the direct products of the territory occupied by the city of London, cannot be made to increase with greater rapidity than that of an arithmetical progression :

Hence it may be affirmed with certainty at any given moment, that the period must very shortly arrive when the population of the city of London will be distressed for want of provisions.

As this conclusion might have been drawn with the same force at any preceding epoch in the history of the city, as at the present, it would follow that the distress must have been regularly increasing for at least a thousand years, and must naturally have become by this time very poignant and oppressive.

Independently of the error in the first of these premises, in regard to the power of increase in the population of the city of London, it is obvious that the notorious falsehood of the conclusion results immediately from the implied supposition, that the inhabitants of this city must subsist of necessity upon the fruits of the soil they occupy; while, as every one knows, this territory, upon which more than a million persons are supported in ease and abundance, does not supply perhaps, directly, the means of subsistence for twenty.

In like manner the error in the argument may be shown, by applying it to the case of an individual; as for example, to that of Mr. Malthus itself. He informs us in one of his works, that he is not a landholder; and he cannot of course derive his means of subsistence from the products of his own soil. His existence therefore demonstrates the falsehood of his system : and if the theory of the Essay on Population were true, its author could never have lived to write it.

On the supposition of the truth of this system of Malthus, the population of every part of the globe would be regulated exactly by the supply of the means of subsistence, and would not any where either fall below or rise above it. As it happens, however, this is no where the case ; and it would, perhaps, be difficult to produce a single example of a territory in which the population is determined exactly by the products of the soil, and neither falls below nor rises above the precise number of persons which these products are capable of subsisting. Mr. Malthus has noticed himself a very large class of cases in which the population falls below the means of subsistence ; and has accounted for their existence upon principles just in themselves, but wholly at variance with his own theory, as I shall have occasion to show hereafter. The large class of cases in which the population rises above the means of subsistence, and which is still more fatal to his system than the other, he has wholly overlooked, and has not even made an attempt to account for. This class of

cases includes all cities, many rich and extensive provinces, as for instance that of Holland
at the time of its highest prosperity, and even
some independent states, as the kingdoms of
Sweden and Norway, which derive from abroad
a part of their supply of provisions. Any one
of these instances is completely ruinous to the
system of Malthus: for whatever reasons may
be given why the population does not reach in
particular cases the standard fixed by the supply
of provisions, it is evident that there can be no
exception on the other side until a method shall
be discovered of living without food.

Having thus pointed out the most obvious
error in the celebrated argument of the comparison of ratios, I shall proceed in the next
chapter to consider the real power of increase
in the human species, and to examine the correctness of the assumption of Mr. Malthus in
regard to this subject.

CHAPTER V.

On the Power of Increase in the Human Species.

In the refutation of the main argument of Mr. Malthus, which has been attempted in the preceding chapter, I have taken for granted both his preliminary propositions in regard to the rates of increase of population and of food; and have shown, I think, satisfactorily, that, even on this supposition, his conclusion is entirely erroneous. But this supposition is far from being correct: and of the two preliminary propositions or premises, the one which states the rate of increase of the human species, involves another material error, sufficient of itself, and independently of the objection developed in the preceding chapter, to vitiate completely the author's conclusion.

The abstract theory of perfectibility ascribes all the evils we suffer to the existence or the abuses of political institutions; and maintains, that by the abolition or reform of these institutions, their consequences, physical and moral evil, would of course disappear entirely. To this it is objected, that as physical and moral evil are the only known checks upon the progress of population, the removal of these checks would be followed by a rapid and indefinite increase of the species, until the whole earth would be finally overpeopled. If, in order to present this objection in a more definite shape, we attempt to make a statement of the actual rate of increase that might be expected under such circumstances, it is evident, that the highest rate which has ever been known actually to occur, will be a very low calculation : because the supposition is, that the ordinary checks on the progress of population are removed ; and however favorable may have been the circumstances under which its highest known rate of increase was observed, it must still have taken place under the operation, to a greater or less degree, of the ordinary checks. The population of the United States of America, which affords the instance in question, however favorably situated, has by no means been wholly exempt from the influence of moral and physical evil. Hence, for the purpose of refuting the abstract theory of Mr. Godwin, the rate of increase assumed by Mr. Malthus, upon the authority of the example of the United States, is not an exaggerated estimate, but, on the contrary, is far below the truth. But for the main purpose for which Mr. Malthus employs this estimate, namely, that of ascertaining the proportion existing in reality between the rate of increase of population under all its ordinary checks, and that of the means of subsistence, it is evident, that the estimate in question is as much too high, as it is in the other case too low.

With a view of refuting the theory of Godwin, we assume the truth of his conclusion, that physical and moral evil, the ordinary checks on the progress of population, have ceased to exist. When we wish to discover the real relation between the rates of increase of population and of food, we must take into consideration all the checks to which the increase of either is subject.

To assume the highest known rate of increase that has ever been observed as the standard of the ordinary progress of population, would be like assuming the strength and intelligence of the most powerful and wisest man that ever existed as the standard of the ordinary intellectual and physical endowments of the race. It is evi-

dent that in this case it would be unsafe to draw
a general conclusion from a single instance ; and
that the single instances least suitable for this
purpose would be precisely those of the highest
and of the lowest known rates of increase ; the
former of which has been selected by Mr. Malthus.   The proper course would be to inquire,
first, what is the natural power of increase in
the human species ? secondly, what are the
checks, ordinary and extraordinary, that oppose
the developement of this power ? and, lastly,
what is the real rate of increase which we observe to occur in fact under the operation of
these checks?   Having ascertained in this way
the true rate at which population actually
increases under any given circumstances ; and
having also ascertained the pinciples that regulate the supply of provisions, we may establish
with safety a comparison between the respective
rates of increase of population and of food, and
may calculate the probability, under any given
circumstances, of the occurrence of abundance
or scarcity.

Mr. Malthus, on the contrary, has not even
attempted to calculate the real rate at which
population increases under the operation of all

the natural checks. His assumption is therefore entirely gratuitous : and if it were correct, it could only be by a lucky chance. In reality, however, it is not only gratuitous, but wholly false : and, what is somewhat remarkable, the work of Mr. Malthus himself contains a complete and satisfactory refutation of it, forming one of the longest and most valuable sections of the Essay. A little explanation will show the reader at once the nature of this refutation, and the way in which Mr. Malthus was led unconsciously to furnish it himself.

Having established, to his own satisfaction, on abstract grounds, the principle, that population has a tendency every where to go beyond the supply of provisions, and in fact presses hard against it, Mr. Malthus naturally looks round the world to see how far his doctrine is confirmed by experience, and finds that almost every known case is, in one way or another, at variance with it. The United States of America, which furnish his rule in regard to the rate of increase, confute his conclusion, by also furnishing the example of the most abundant supply of provisions that has ever been known. On the contrary, in many barbarous communities, where population is actually diminishing, there is much suffering from actual want. In a large class of cases, the population actually exceeds very much the number of persons which could be subsisted from the direct products of the soil occupied by it, and yet lives in abundance. In another large class the population falls in greater or less degrees below the number that might be supported from the direct products of the soil, and feels of course no apprehension of a scarcity. In few if any instances do we see any symptoms of this necessary and universal famine, excepting under the precise circumstances in which it was least of all to be expected on the author's principles, to wit, among the barbarous tribes where population is actually declining.

Of these several classes of instances, all in different ways adverse to the theory he has attempted to establish, Mr. Malthus seems to have been principally struck with those in which the population falls short of the number which the products of the soil would easily support; and in which, although the country is well peopled, there is no suffering, unless by accident, from actual famine. This is in fact the situation of almost all the civilised nations on the globe : and Mr. Malthus has endeavored to account for the possibility of it by examining in detail the particular circumstances of most of these nations, with a view of proving that the population is here kept below its natural level by the operation of moral and physical evil : and in each particular case he points out the particular forms of evil which produce this result. The reasoning of Mr. Malthus in this part of the Essay is just and conclusive : but he does not seem to have observed that it overthrows entirely one of the two preliminary propositions upon which the whole fabric of his system is founded. This will appear very plainly by stating the two arguments in a simple and concise form.

The human race, says Mr. Malthus in the first chapter of the Essay, has the power of increasing its numbers in the manner of a geometrical progression :

But the necessary means of subsistence can only be increased in the manner of an arithmetical progression :

Therefore there is a constant tendency in every part of the world towards an excess of population and a scarcity of food.

But, says the same writer in the subsequent part of the Essay now alluded to, there is in point of fact no example of a nation in which the populaton is not kept below the level of the means of subsistence by the operation of moral and physical evil :

Therefore the human race, under the operation of these checks, has not the power of increasing its numbers in the manner of a geometrical progression :

Therefore there is no tendency in any part of the world towards an excess of population and a scarcity of food.

Both these arguments rest alike upon the authority of Mr. Malthus ; it is sufficiently clear that the latter of them completely refutes the former, and leaves it no force whatever, excepting as an answer to the abstract system of perfectibility, which supposes the non-existence of evil.

Mr. Malthus has, however, contrived to reconcile the two arguments with each other in his own mind in such a way that he appears to be fully convinced of the correctness of both : and even considers the conclusions of both as applicable to the same communities at the same time.

He holds, in other words, that the same nation has and has not, at a given moment, a tendency towards an excess of population and scarcity of food. Take for example the kingdom of France. Mr. Malthus maintains that the natural power of the human race to increase its numbers in the manner of a geometrical progression, is checked in that country by the operation of certain moral and physical causes. The necessary consequence from this position is, that the human race does not possess in that country the power of increasing its numbers in the manner supposed, and that the danger of scarcity deduced by Mr. Malthus from the existence of this power does not occur in France. It would seem then that France, or any other country thus situated, must be treated as an exception to the general rule, even on the principles of Mr. Malthus himself. Far from it. Mr. Malthus holds, on the contrary, that the population still presses hard against the means of subsistence, in the same cases in which he asserts at the same time, that it is kept below the means of subsistence by the operation of moral and physical checks.

Mr. Malthus might perhaps reply to this objection, that there is no inconsistency in assuming the power of increase to be rapid and indefinite, except as far as it is checked by a want of the means of subsistence, and then stating that the same power is actually limited, in a great variety of cases, by the various forms of physical and moral evil ; because these various forms, in their effect upon population, all resolve themselves into a want of the means of subsistence, and therefore the check upon the power of increase is in both statements precisely the same. But this reply admits of the obvious answer, that if the power of increase is subject by the laws of our nature to be checked by an accidental want of subsistence, resulting from the influence of moral and physical evil, before it is checked by a necessary want arising from the exhaustion of the resources of the earth, or any part of it, then it is necessary, in order to ascertain the rate of increase, for the purpose of comparing it with the possible resources of the soil, to take into view the effects of this prior and accidental check. The population of Turkey, for example, is subject to the check of tyranny. If then we wish to know how fast it is likely to increase, and whether it will probably ever exhaust the resources of the soil, we cannot assume an indefinite power of increase in the population, and compare it with a limited power of production in the soil ; but we must inquire first what are the resources of the territory, and then what is the power of increase in a population subject to the check of tyranny. Whether this check operates by producing a premature and accidental scarcity, or in any other way, is of no importance.

The power of increase in the human species, taken in general, is therefore the natural power of increase limited by the checks resulting from the moral and physical imperfections of our nature, whether they operate in the form of scarcity, or in any other way. If it were the object of an inquirer to ascertain the extent of this power by examples, it would be necessary to examine all the known cases in connexion with the circumstances under which they occurred, and to deduce a mean number from the whole. To assume any single example as a standard, would be clearly a vicious mode of reasoning ; and, as I observed before, the instances least suitable for this purpose would be precisely those of the highest and lowest known rates. As I have endeavored to show in some of the preceding chapters, that the increase of population is the principle of abundance and not of scarcity, it is unnecessary for the present purpose to inquire what the real power of increase is. Nevertheless, as the subject is interesting, and as it has generally been examined in connexion with the question which I have undertaken to discuss, I shall offer a few remarks upon it in the two succeeding chapters.

CHAPTER VI.

On the Causes that Determine the Extent of Population.

I⊤ is a part of the system of Mr. Malthus, that the extent of population is regulated by the supply of the means of subsistence. This proposition is not, however, directly made out, either by argument or induction ; but is merely a corollary from the comparison of ratios, upon which his whole theory is founded. As the population on this system must of necessity overtake the supply of provisions, and cannot outstrip it by the condition of our nature, it will of course be determined or regulated by it.

If the objections which I have advanced in the two preceding chapters against the argument of the comparison of ratios are well founded, this conclusion, as well as the others which Mr. Malthus has drawn from that argument, falls of itself. The principle has also been refuted in another form in the second and third chapters, where I have shown that the supply of provisions

in every country is determined by the extent
and character of the population, and of course
that the proposition is not only incorrect, but
directly contrary to the truth. I have also had
occasion to observe in the preceding chapter,
that Mr. Malthus himself admits, that there are
very few if any instances in which his theory is
confirmed by experience. As far, therefore, as
there is any foundation for the general principles maintained in this Essay, the assertion that
population is regulated by the supply of provisions has already been sufficiently refuted.
Before I proceed to inquire into the causes that
really produce this effect, I propose, however, to
add a few explanatory remarks in regard to this
part of the theory of Mr. Malthus.

If by the assertion, that population is regulated by the supply of provisions, it were merely
intended to be intimated that a quantity of provisions actually existing at any given moment,
will not afford a competent support to a much
larger number of persons than those by whose
labor it was procured, and for whose use it was
intended, the proposition is no doubt very obviously true, in its application both to individuals
and communities, but is of no value in political

science. It is certain that if I am surprised at dinner-time by half a dozen friends, when I have only provided for my own family, the entertainment they find will be scanty. In like manner, if, by miracle, a large number of additional guests should present themselves, at once, without giving previous notice, at the great banquet of nature, they would find, to use the phrase of Mr. Malthus, that no place had been provided for them. But miracles are not the subject of consideration in political economy ; and the natural order of events has been so regulated by the great Dispenser of this banquet, that no additional guest can ever present himself, until timely notice has been given of his coming, and ample provision made for his reception.

If by the assertion alluded to it be meant, that the supply of the means of subsistence which any country is capable of affording is a fixed quantity, which can only support a given number of persons, to which number the population must of course be limited, it may be remarked in answer, that if the quantity of provisions which a country is able to afford be a fixed one, there must be some cause to fix it, and that on the system of Mr. Malthus no such cause can be assigned. If instead of supposing the supply of the means of subsistence to be regulated, as it really is, by the extent and character of the population, we reverse the order of cause and effect, and suppose the extent and character of the population to be regulated by the supply of the means of subsistence; no imaginable cause remains by which the latter can be determined, unless it be the influence of soil and climate. But this cause is wholly insufficient to account for the effect, because we find, that under the same circumstances of soil and climate, the same countries afford at different and even at the same periods, the most various quantities of the means of subsistence. If the supply of the means of provisions were fixed by the nature of the soil and climate, or by any cause other than the extent and character of the population, we should regularly find all the different races of men inhabiting any given country equally well supplied with the comforts of life, and increasing or diminishing in number in the same way. In point of fact, however, most large countries contain, at the same time and under the same circumstances of soil and climate, various races of men very differently situated in regard to the circumstances above mentioned. North America affords at present a striking illustration of this remark. There is a race of men to be found upon it, whose numbers do not at present exceed at the utmost a few hundred thousands, and are constantly and rapidly diminishing. Few as they are, and scattered over the vast extent of a boundless and most productive continent, they are nevertheless unable, by incessant and unremitted labor, and by exposure to inconceivable hardships and dangers, to obtain a sufficient supply of the ordinary comforts and necessaries of life. On the same continent, and in the same circumstances of soil and climate, another race of men obtains, by moderate labor and very trifling personal sacrifices, an ample and luxurious subsistence, for a rapidly increasing population of more than ten millions. Upon any theory, excepting that which supposes the supply of provisions to be determined by the extent and character of the population, such a difference as this is wholly unaccountable.

In reality, however, Mr. Malthus would not probably maintain the proposition, that population is regulated by the supply of provisions, in

either of the precise senses alluded to above.
His doctrine is, that without inquiry into the
causes that regulate the supply of provisions,
and supposing this supply to attain the maximum which the laws of nature render possible,
the power of increase is so active, that population will still overtake the means of subsistence,
and tend strongly to outstrip them. Hence the
true answer to this part of the theory of Mr.
Malthus is furnished by the objections in the
two preceding chapters to the argument of the
comparison of ratios. The remarks which I
have now made may serve however to indicate a
deficiency in the system of this writer, even
admitting the correctness of his leading principles. If population is determined by the supply of the means of subsistence, it remains for
Mr. Malthus to point out by what cause the
supply of those means of subsistence is determined ; and why, of two races of men equally
favored in every point of natural situation, one
is pining and perishing with actual want, and
the other revelling in plenty, and supplying from
its abundance the necessities of half the nations
on the globe.

CHAPTER VII.

The same Subject continued.

THE reality of a considerable power of increase in the human species is too obvious a fact to be called in question, and is admitted by all the writers who have treated this subject. The absolute extent of this power is variously stated by different authors. Mr. Malthus, resting on the authority of the example of the United States, affirms that the human race has the power of doubling its numbers at least once in twenty-five years. Mr. Godwin denies the correctness of the accounts given of the increase of population in the United States ; but affirms, on the authority of what he considers a better attested instance, that of Sweden, that the power of increase is competent to the doubling of a population once in about a century.

For the purposes of general reasoning, it is evident that the theory is in both cases precisely the same. Both suppositions admit a considerable power of increase, capable, if not counteracted, of overstocking the earth with inhabitants at no very remote period. The theory of Godwin also admits, like that of Malthus, that the operation of the unchecked power of increase, would be in the manner of a geometrical progression. If the population of the kingdom of Sweden was one million in the year 1700, and two millions a century after, it will amount, on the principles of Mr. Godwin, to four millions in the year 1900, and to eight in the year 2000: and would thus proceed in the manner of the series of numbers 1. 2. 4. 8. &c. which is a geometrical progression. It is rather singular that Mr. Godwin should not have perceived, that in contesting this part of the system of Mr. Malthus, he was in fact contradicting one of his own leading principles.

As these two writers and the public in general are agreed in regard to the theory of the absolute power of increase, so they also admit, with equal unanimity, that this power of increase is checked in its developement, and does not produce in reality its natural and complete effect. Although the population of the United States has doubled itself for a length of time every twenty-five years, and although that of Sweden, and some other countries in Europe, appears to be doubling itself about once in a century, it is acknowledged, that the population of the globe has not, taken together, been increasing at this rate during the period of which we have an historical account; and it even seems doubtful, whether it is at all greater now than it was three or four thousand years ago. It is acknowledged, that in many parts of the earth population has been stationary for long periods of time : and that in others it has rapidly diminished, and is still diminishing. As no effect can happen without some adequate cause, it follows therefore, that as there is, by the admission of all, an active power of increase in the species, so there must be, by the admission of all, some active causes in operation of a contrary nature that tend to check it.

As Godwin and Malthus are agreed upon these preliminary points, so they also agree in regard to the character of the immediate causes that produce the effect in question. It is granted by both and by all other inquirers, that these immediate causes are the various forms of physical and moral evil. It is only in assigning the remote origin of these immediate causes, that the theories begin to differ. Mr. Malthus, as we have seen, ascribes them to a constant and universal excess of population resulting necessarily from a standing law of nature. Mr. Godwin, on the contrary, traces them to the influence of vicious political institutions. The inherent errors of the theory of Malthus, which accounts for the depression of population by supposing its excess, have been already pointed out. That of Godwin is, thus far, more just and plausible, inasmuch as vicious political institutions are among the most active and operative forms of evil. But the theory is radically erroneous, because it exactly reverses the order of cause and effect. Vicious political institutions are not the causes but the consequences of the existence of moral and physical evil, and are among the forms in which these causes operate. If man were a being incapable by nature of vice or error, it is obvious that the political institutions formed by him, like all his other works, would be perfect. The original imperfection of our constitution, and the existence of a principle of evil, are therefore the final causes to which we must trace the faults of political institutions, as well as the other forms of vice and error. Hence we see the error of Mr. Godwin's deduction, that the abolition of political institutions would bring about a state of perfect innocence and happiness. This would be true, if bad government were the sole and original principle of evil; since with the non-existence of the cause, the effect of course would cease. But the error is obvious, when we consider vicious institutions as only one of the various forms of evil; since if evil should cease to exist in this form by the abolition, or which indeed is a much more likely way of producing the effect, by the highest possible improvement of these institutions, it would still display itself in the various and innumerable shapes in which it appears under the name of individual error and vice.

In order to rectify the theories of Godwin and Malthus, in regard to the nature of the causes which counteract the progress of population, it is only necessary to take the point in which they are both agreed, to wit, that the immediate checks on population are the various forms of moral and physical evil; and rejecting their attempts to trace the principle of evil to some other original cause, to consider it as itself an original ingredient in the constitution of the universe. An earthquake swallows up the whole population of a large city. This is not the effect of bad government, nor of any disproportion between the ratios that regulate the increase of provisions and of population. It results from the existence of earthquakes as a part of the order of nature. A furious conqueror ravages at the head of his troops a civilised and populous territory, and massacres a considerable part of its inhabitants. This is not the effect of vicious institutions, or of an excess of population, but of the possibility in the order of nature of the occurrence of individual vice in this horrid form. The principle of evil is therefore the original as well as the immediate check upon the increase of the human race : as the social feelings to which we owe this increase are acknowledged by all to be the principle of good. Population and depopulation are the forms in which good and evil, virtue and vice, happiness and misery, exercise their operation upon man : and wherever we find the effect, we are sure to find it attended by the corresponding cause, population by virtue and happiness, and depopulation by misery and vice.

As the various persons and parties that differ in opinion upon the controverted questions discussed in the present work are all agreed in thinking, that the immediate practical checks upon the progress of population are moral and physical evil, it is unnecessary to enlarge upon this point for the purpose of proving it. It may be proper, however, to complete the general view here given of the subject, by specifying the principal forms under which these causes operate in producing the effect supposed. These forms may be conveniently reduced to four general heads. 1. Physical evil, wholly independent of human agency, or casualties. 2. Private vice. 3. Vicious political institutions. 4. Barbarism. I shall add a few observations upon each of these classes, inverting the order in which they are here named.

1. Barbarism: This form of evil might perhaps be considered as belonging to the class of vicious political institutions. But for reasons given in a preceding chapter, I regard it as an imperfect and unnatural state, and the scanty fractions of the race that are found in it as hardly entitled to the name of moral beings. The distinguishing character of this state of society is

the employment of insufficient methods of obtaining subsistence ; and the resort to agriculture, as the principal means for effecting this
purpose, draws, as I have observed in a preceding chapter, the distinguishing line between the
barbarous and civilised states. All other modes,
such as hunting, fishing, and the keeping of
flocks and herds, afford so precarious and scanty
a supply of necessaries, as not to admit of any
increase of population. Under the pressure of
continual hardships and want, the increase of
the inhabitants is checked in every possible way.
Marriages are unproductive from the excessive
toil and suffering to which the parties are exposed. The same causes sweep off a great part of
the children that are born in infancy, and thin
the numbers of the small portion that arrive at
maturity. In every community where agriculture is not the principal means of obtaining subsistence, the population will probably be found
to be diminishing with greater or less rapidity.
The rude political institutions that exist in this
state of society are necessarily of the worst kind,
and private vice prevails in its most atrocious
and disgusting forms ; but the radical defect is
a vicious economical system, which at once lies

at the root of all the immediate evils, and renders improvement impossible.

2. The civilised or agricultural state affords the possibility of a regular and rapid increase of population. We find, however, that such regular and rapid increase is far from being universal, and that there are other forms of moral and physical evil, which produce in this state of society an effect, less powerful indeed, but analogous in its operation to the vicious economical system that forms the counteracting principle in barbarous tribes. Of these various forms it can hardly be doubted, that vicious political institutions, from the permanent and extensive influence which they exercise, are among the most effective. Where the vices of these institutions are notorious and glaring, as for example in Turkey, the advantages of society are exclusively in the hands of a very small number of persons, and the mass of the people are exposed to nearly the same hardships and suffering as in a state of absolute barbarism. Their moral and intellectual character is equally degraded, and the increase of population is checked to nearly the same extent. Hence, in Turkey, and in most of the Mahometan countries, population appears

to have been, for a long time, in a regular course of diminution. In most of the Christian countries of Europe, the political institutions, though vicious in greater or less degrees, still afford, to a certain extent, protection to the personal rights of the whole mass of society. In such a situation there is opportunity for industry, and for the developement of valuable intellectual and moral qualities, or in other words, for the progress of civilisation, and the increase of numbers. We find accordingly, that in most of these countries population appears to have been, for a long time, gradually though slowly increasing; and especially within the two or three last centuries, during which the improvement of political institutions and the progress of civilisation have been most remarkable. This increase of population is most perceptible in the states which are best governed and most civilised, as in England, France, and Germany. Beside the regular operation of vicious political institutions, in checking the progress of population by degrading the character and condition of the mass of the people, the frequent wars which they naturally produce have a still more direct tendency towards the same point.

3. Private vice : The operation of individual vices, such as indolence, improvidence, and sensuality, in counteracting the power of increase, is too obvious to require any explanation. These are probably the checks that operate with most force in long settled and thickly peopled countries, as for example in China and Japan, where the government is mild, and the means of subsistence abundant, but where there are evidently some causes in operation which prevent the population from increasing very fast, perhaps, not at all. In the savage state, where the life of man is a perpetual warfare with all the elements and animals that surround him—where constant suffering hardens the heart, and exasperates the temper—the prevailing vices are ferocity and contempt for the happiness of others. In the bosom of civilised society, where existence is joyous and easy, these qualities disappear : but the imperfection of our nature displays itself in a train of softer vices, less offensive and odious in their character than those of barbarism, but probably very effectual in their operation as checks on the increase of the species. We are too little acquainted with the history of the great eastern empires above mentioned, to know pre-

cisely what the state of population is, much less
to decide with certainty upon the causes that
regulate it.   There is however room to suppose,
that vicious political institutions, as well as private immorality, have some operation in producing this effect.

4. Physical evils, wholly independent of the
agency of man, such as earthquakes, inunda-
tions, epidemic diseases, the accidental failure
of crops, and other occurrences of this description, must also be reckoned among the active
checks on the progress of population.   The
operation of this class of checks is of course
entirely irregular, and probably much less considerable than that of any of the others.

Such are the principal forms of moral and
physical evil which neutralize the power of
increase at the various stages in the progress of
civilisation.   What then do we gain, it may be
asked, by the improvements of our economical
or political systems, if they only serve to substitute one sort of vice for another ?   The answer
to this question, though obvious, is quite satisfactory.

1. In the first place we gain for a given territory a great increase of human beings suscepti-

ble of enjoyment and capable of virtue; and their situation is, in point of fact, superior and happier in proportion to the degree of their civilisation. The inhabitants of a city in the United States are not without their imperfections, their vices, and their sufferings; but their condition is certainly every way preferable to that of a tribe of the neighboring Indians, or a village of Russian slaves. Here then is a great positive acquisition of human life and human happiness.

2. The vices most frequent in a state of civilisation are not necessary or irremediable in any given degree, but may be indefinitely diminished by the continual progress of civilisation and improvement; although, as I have already observed, they can never be entirely removed. It is the tendency of good institutions to substitute industry and activity in the room of sensuality and indolence among the mass of the people. In proportion to the improvement of the public morals, population would continue to advance with proportional rapidity; and this advance would not be attended with any danger of scarcity, but, as I think I have shown in a

preceding chapter, would be a powerful principle of abundance until the whole earth should be overpeopled : an event which, as Mr. Malthus justly observes, is too remote to be a subject of reasonable apprehension.

CHAPTER VIII.

On the Increase of Population in the United States of America.

THE United States of America furnish the most remarkable example of a rapid increase of population that has yet appeared in any age or country. From the time of the first settlement of their territory two hundred years ago up to the present day, the number of their inhabitants has regularly doubled itself at least as often as once in twenty-five years. Mr. Godwin, it is true, ascribes this extraordinary increase, in a great measure, to the effect of emigration from Europe ; but in the attempt to substantiate this assertion he has failed completely. His calculations, in regard to the amount of the emigration into the United States, are entirely at variance with all the most authentic statistical accounts ; and the argument upon which he principally seems to rely, drawn from a comparison of the two enumerations of 1800 and 1810, involves an error which evidently destroys its force. It is true that the number of persons over ten years of age given in the census of 1810, must be the same with the whole number of inhabitants given in that of 1800, deducting the deaths which occurred between these two periods ; and it is also true that on the calculations of the amount of this mortality contained in the work of Mr. Godwin, there would remain a very great difference between the two numbers to be accounted for by emigration. But these calculations are founded on the very obviously false supposition, that the mortality among that part of the population over one or two years of age, is as great in proportion, as it is among the whole population taken together. This palpable error being corrected, and the real mortality estimated from the surest accounts, and the most probable conjectures, the conclusions drawn from a comparison of the enumerations according to the method of Mr. Booth agree very well with the best statistical documents. It appears from all these sources of information, that the number of emigrants has, at no period since the first settlement of the country, been considerable enough to produce any material effect upon the state of population. The rapid augmentation of numbers that has taken place is therefore the result of the natural power of increase operating under circumstances more favorable than have hitherto been known in any other country.

As the various forms of moral and physical evil are admitted by all to be the only checks on the progress of population, it follows of course, that they must be less felt in the United States than in any other part of the world. In the preceding chapter, I have attempted to arrange these forms under several principal heads; and it may not be uninteresting to take a rapid review of the actual situation of the United States in reference to this arrangement. If it be correct, we may expect to find the operation of the several classes of checks which I have enumerated less considerable in the United States than elsewhere.

Of these checks, the one first mentioned, that of barbarism, has of course no operation in an agricultural and civilised community.

The fourth, comprehending physical evils, independent of human agency, is far from being wholly unfelt. Accidental famine, it is true, is quite unknown: but epidemical and other diseases, not resulting immediately from intemperance, prevail in the United States to a considerable extent. The principal cities in the southern section are regularly visited by the yellow fever; but as this scourge is limited in its operation to the inhabitants of three or four not very populous places, the actual mortality resulting from it is not very great. But independently of the yellow fever, the inhabitants of the whole interior part of the country suffer from diseases occasioned by the unwholesome exhalations that arise from a rich and humid soil, opened for the first time to the influence of the sun. The eastern and middle states, which have long been settled, and are now pretty well cleared, and comparatively populous, are the only ones which can be considered as positively healthy. And as the most rapid increase of population takes place in the new states, it is plain that it cannot be accounted for by the supposition of an uncommonly salubrious climate. In fact there are probably few parts of Europe in which the check of diseases not resulting from intemperance or want is felt so strongly as it is in the United States.

There are also other checks belonging to this class that have always operated very powerfully from the first settlement of the country up to the present day. The physical hardships endured by the inhabitants of the United States, have probably been greater than any civilised community was ever compelled to struggle with before. The first settlers founded their establishments in the midst of a hardy and ferocious race of savages, with whom they were forced to carry on a perpetual war of life and death. As the population increased, the savages retired into the interior ; but the enterprising emigrants from the new states, as they gradually pushed forward the European settlements, always did it with the tomahawk and scalping knife impending over their heads. The rapid decay of these tribes, and their growing respect for the government of the United States, have at last, in a great measure, relieved the country from this scourge, except in time of war with Great Britain, a power whose government considers the horrors of savage hostility as a very honorable and useful engine to employ against a Christian and civilised enemy.

Independently of the inconvenience of waging a perpetual war with the savages, the other hardships naturally incident to the exploring of a new country are far from being slight. The labor, to which the first settlers in a wilderness are exposed, is excessive, and their privations almost insupportable. The emigrant goes out into the woods with no resources but his axe and his gun. He has no shelter from the weather till he has built him a house of the trees that were growing when he arrived; and he plants his first crop of corn among the stumps of the forest which he has hewn or burnt down to make room for it. He has no hope of a competent provision for the close of his life, except such as is founded upon wielding the axe and urging the plough with incessant activity as long as health and strength remain. When we add to these hardships the diseases incident to new settlements, of which I have already spoken, it must be allowed that the physical situation of their inhabitants is far from being particularly favorable. It is evidently therefore not to the absence of merely physical checks that we are to trace the unprecedented increase of population in the United States : and we must rather look for it in the comparatively lighter pressure of moral evil in its two principal forms of vicious political institutions and private vice.

We find accordingly, upon reference to the situation of the United States, that the checks of population arising from both these causes, are probably less considerable than they ever were in any other country. The object of good government, that is, the security of personal and national rights, is completely attained; and with as small sacrifices on the part of individuals, in the various forms of taxes, military service, or acquiescence in restraints on their industry, as can well be imagined possible; much smaller certainly than were ever made before for the same purpose in other communities. The check resulting from vicious institutions may therefore be regarded as absolutely null.

Various circumstances also unite to render the check resulting from private vice less considerable than in most other countries. From the combined effect of the character of our institutions and the state of property, there is no country in which the importance of individuals in the community is so great as it is with us. By far the greater part of the citizens are proprietors of land; and the laborer, from the facility with which he can become a proprietor if he pleases, is nearly as independent and as important as the proprietor himself. Almost every citizen possesses political rights ; and takes a part, in one form or another, in the government of the country. These circumstances naturally give to the individual a sense of his own dignity and value ; and tend to produce, in the first place, attention to his own interest, or habits of foresight and industry, and, secondly, intelligence, or the capacity of promoting his own interest, and that of his family and connexions. One of the consequences of such habits and feelings is a comparatively slight pressure upon the mass of the people, of the diseases and sufferings that are the natural effects of improvidence, idleness, and vicious habits.

To these causes for the comparative absence of private vice may be added the nature of the employment most general among the people, and the thinness of the population. Agriculture, the almost universal occupation of the citizens of the United States, is generally regarded as more favorable to good morals and to health than any other whatever. The soft and sensual vices, that naturally grow up in the soil of a dense population, and probably act as the principal check on the increase of man in the later periods of the progress of society, are in a great measure unknown. The mass of the inhabitants are thinly scattered over a boundless territory; and if they lose the ease and joyousness that form the charm of life in more populous communities, they are free, in compensation, from the vice and disease to which such communities are subject. Their happiness is of a chaste and serious cast. Abundance is within the reach of all; and the prevalent habits and institutions naturally inspire all with an ardent wish to obtain it. But this can only be done by a steady course of labor continued unremittingly through the active part of life. Temperance and industry are therefore the general characteristics of the inhabitants of the United States; and their principal relaxations are found in the quiet comforts of the domestic circle. They know but little of the thoughtless mirth and the joyous light-heartedness that prevail in some other countries; and if individuals occasionally turn their attention from their immediate concerns, it is probably to fix it upon the still more weighty matters of politics or religion. Whether such a society has a better enjoyment of life

than any other, is a question which we need not
undertake to determine : it is sufficient for the
present purpose to remark, that the habits I have
described are more favorable than any others to
the increase of population.

In one word, the causes of the rapid increase
of population in the United States must be
looked for in their peculiar political and geographical circumstances, in consequence of which
the inhabitants have been able to take advantage
of the improved moral habits and social institutions which are found in advanced stages of civilisation, without being exposed to the peculiar
evils of immorality, improvidence and indolence,
which in older and more populous countries are
usually, by way of compensation, the natural
products of the same rich soil.

Good government and good morals, or in
other words, the absence of the checks resulting from vicious institutions and private vice,
are therefore the main causes of this remarkable phenomenon. We are authorised to draw
this conclusion from actual observations on the
situation of the country : and there is also no
way of accounting for the fact in question, but
by the supposition that the checks on population

resulting from the pressure of moral evil are comparatively small, since, as we have seen, the check of immediate physical evil is probably quite as severe as in most other civilised countries.

Here then, it may be remarked *en passant*, we have a short and decisive answer to the calumnies on the moral character of the citizens of the United States, in which some European writers are accustomed to indulge. When the judicious travellers, and still more judicious critics of the mother country, think proper to gratify their spleen by representing us as an indolent, immoral, and irreligious people, we have only to refer them to the census for a complete mathematical demonstration of the folly and falsehood of their assertions.

CHAPTER IX.

On the Policy of encouraging Marriage.

IF the system of Mr. Malthus were correct, and the power of increase were, as he supposes, the real and original principle of all the evil we suffer, the only possible hope of any improvement in the state of society would be founded upon an attempt to check the operation of this power by artificial means in one way or another. Some conclusions, that necessarily follow from these premises, can hardly be very agreeable to persons of correct judgment and good feelings. It is certain, for example, that on the supposition of Mr. Malthus, many proceedings of the most inhuman and immoral character, such as the exposure of infants and the promiscuous intercourse of the sexes, would be in the highest degree favorable to the general good. Without enlarging upon this objection, which however is one of very great importance, it may be proper to notice in a brief manner the plan which Mr.

Malthus himself proposes for diminishing the activity of the principle of increase.

This author considers it as a clearly immoral act in any individual to marry without a reasonable prospect of being able to provide for his family ; but does not conceive that the society, to which he belongs, have a right to prevent him from so doing. Whatever good can be done, must therefore be effected by the spontaneous action of individuals. The plan of Mr. Malthus is, that the public authorities should invite and encourage the people to abstain from marrying under the circumstances just mentioned, and should assure them explicitly that if they do it, it must be at their own risk and peril ; that they are responsible for the consequences, whatever they may be ; and that if they or their families come to want, they have no relief to expect from the bounty of society. As a part of this system, all public provision for the poor, the aged, and the infirm, is to be gradually abolished ; and charity, in all the acceptations of the word, to become a dead letter, unless when it may occasionally lead to the relief of an individual case of distress.

Such is the plan which Mr. Malthus himself recommends as being naturally suggested by his own theory. If his enemy had written a book, he certainly could not have presented the system under a more revolting aspect. Still it must be allowed, that if the truth of the general theory be admitted, these measures, or some others of a similar tendency, would really become expedient. Mr. Malthus has therefore proved the firmness and honesty of his character, by thus pursuing his system into all its consequences, however odious and unnatural. I must confess, however, that even on his own supposition of facts, his reasoning in regard to the most expedient remedy for the evil in question does not seem to me to be quite correct : and there are other measures of the same general tendency, that appear to be at once more effectual and equitable than those which he proposes.

It is doubtless very evident, as Mr. Malthus affirms, that it is a clearly immoral act for an individual to marry without a reasonable prospect of being able to support a family : but the principle, that society has no right to prevent him from doing this, does not seem to be equally certain. It is obvious, on the contrary, that as man was intended by nature for a social being, all his personal rights are limited by the general good ; and that no individual can possess any, the exercise of which would be inconsistent with this object. If acts of the kind above mentioned happened only now and then by way of exception, or if the immorality of them were of a nature to produce but little practical injury to society, it might be inexpedient to adopt any prohibitory measures in regard to them: not because society would not have a right so to do, but because the trouble of carrying such a law into execution might be a greater evil than the one to be remedied. But since, on the theory of Mr. Malthus, a large portion of every community are placed by the law of nature under a constant temptation to take this course; and since this precise species of immorality is the one to which all our sufferings and vices must be traced as to a fountain head; it is clearly not only the right but the bounden and indispensable duty of governments to make such laws as may serve most effectually to remedy the evil. The care of providing the necessary check cannot be left with safety to individuals, since those of the poorer sort, who compose the mass of the people, are wholly unable to judge of the necessity of any such measures; and if they even saw the danger, are under the immediate influ-

ence of a strong natural tendency, which would
lead them to overlook the obligation of providing against it. To the magistrates, therefore,
who see the evil, and have no temptation to be
negligent, belongs undoubtedly the duty of preventing it by legislative measures.

This might be done in two ways, either of
which would be effectual, and on the supposition, unobjectionable. A calculation might be
made of the age at which the whole population
might marry without any danger to the society
of an excess of numbers. After this period had
been determined with mathematical exactness, a
law should be passed prohibiting any marriage
between parties who had not arrived at the legal
age. Such a law would be equitable, because
it would operate impartially upon the whole
community. On the system of Mr. Malthus, the
poor, in addition to their other inconveniences,
are required to sacrifice the comforts of domestic life to the general good : and the rich
are invested, beside all their other advantages,
with a monopoly of love and marriage. Such a
plan is neither just nor safe : and the privations
and sufferings, imposed upon communities by
common necessities, must be shared alike by all.

When the crew of a ship are put upon short allowance, the officers, if they do not wish to be massacred, must submit to the same fare with the rest.

Another equally plausible arrangement would be, to calculate with exactness how large a proportion of the community might marry at an early age without any danger of an excess of population, and then to select by lot the requisite number of individuals of the two sexes, and prohibit the rest from marrying at all. Society would then resemble, in this particular, the monarchy of the bees, and would have its queens, its drones, and its laborers. The two former classes would devote their attention to the continuation of the race, while the individuals of the latter were exclusively employed in providing for the comfortable subsistence of the whole. Both these schemes, as it strikes me, are far more plausible, on the supposition of the truth of Mr. Malthus's theory, than the one which he has adopted. If they appear absurd, we may conclude that the suppositions which naturally lead to them are false and groundless.

It is doubtless true, as I have observed already, that it would be an immoral act for a man to marry without a reasonable prospect of being able to support a family. In like manner it would be immoral for a man to eat without a reasonable prospect of being able to digest his food. We are bound to exercise our understandings in the regulation of these parts of our conduct as of every other. But Providence has not made the preservation of life and the continuance of the species to depend upon the mere suggestions of a sense of duty. For the purpose of insuring the accomplishment of these essential objects, the attention of individuals is directed to them by the impulses of strong natural instincts. The instinct of love is the natural motive to marriage. As it is given to every individual, it is evidently the intention of nature that all should marry : and as it is stronger at an early period of life than at any other, it is equally evident that youth was the time intended by nature for the gratification of this instinct in marriage. As a general rule, therefore, the order of nature has provided that all should marry young ; and the accomplishment of this, as of every other law of nature, must tend to promote the general good, at the same time that it advances the happiness of individuals. To this, as to all other laws of nature, there are are doubtless exceptions ; and an individual, whose case happens to form one of the exceptions, or who supposes that it does, is bound to act accordingly. But to affirm that the mass of mankind, in obeying without hesitation the law of nature, indicated by a strong natural instinct, would run any risk of doing injury to themselves or to society, and that such injury could be prevented by acting in each case upon a calculation of probabilities, either supposes that the dictates of feeling and of reason are essentially different, while they are, in fact, only two forms in which the same common law of nature declares itself; or that reason is, with the mass of the people, a surer instrument by which to ascertain the law of nature than feeling ; a proposition too obviously false to be sustained for a moment.

Since then it is provided in the order of nature that all should marry early, we are certain that the general good will be promoted by an obedience to this law. The few exceptions to it, that prudence may render necessary, do not require to be regulated by any legislative proceedings of the nature of those recommended by Mr. Malthus, or suggested above. Any system which affirms that the universal prevalence of early marriages is adverse to the general good, and ought to be checked, is in open contradiction with the certain laws of nature ; and must therefore of necessity be false. Such is the character of that of Mr. Malthus.

The most distinguished legislators and philosophers of ancient and modern times have in general regarded the increase of population as a very desirable thing ; and if the principles which I have endeavored to establish are correct, the laws which have been enacted at various times and in different countries for the encouragement of marriage, were predicated upon a much more correct view of the subject, than that taken by Mr. Malthus. In reality, however, little or nothing can be done by legislation, or in any more indirect way, either for the prevention or the encouragement of marriage. Providence has not left it to the wisdom of politicians, to make arrangements for the continuance of the species : but has recommended it to every individual by a motive that was made and meant to be stronger than any adverse consideration that can present itself in the ordinary course of events. The consequence is, that the mass of the people in all countries and at all periods always have married and always will marry upon their arrival at maturity. They want no legal encouragement to do this ; nor would any prohibitory measures prevent them from doing it. Such measures would be as ineffectual as they are superfluous, on the principles maintained in the present work.

CHAPTER X.

On a Public Provision for the Poor.

On the system of Mr. Malthus, a public provision for the support of the poor, such as now exists in Great Britain, and most other Christian nations, is among the most enormous and wanton impositions with which an unhappy people could possibly be visited : and it would be the imperious and pressing duty of the government of every country, where such a system was established, to abolish it as speedily as possible. If Mr. Malthus be correct in his theory, the community are loaded with an intolerable burden, for no other end but to create and keep in existence an immense mass of poverty and wretchedness ; and thus make themselves miserable for the strange object of making other people so. The abolition of the poor laws is therefore one of the first and most urgent practical measures resulting from the theory of this writer.

If the principles which I have endeavored to establish are correct, the poor laws present themselves under a very different point of view. Population not being regulated by the supply of the means of subsistence ; but, on the contrary, the means of subsistence being determined by the extent and character of the population, a legal provision for the infirm and the aged has no effect in augmenting the number of the inhabitants any further than as it may save a few individuals from a premature death. There is no danger that the expectation of being provided for in the alms-house, will either lead to improvident marriages, or prevent the people from pursuing their occupations with zeal and industry. That the whole mass of the people will marry under any circumstances, is a point which must be calculated upon in every community : and the supposition that the sight of the alms-house will tempt the poor to be improvident and idle, is about as reasonable as it would be to imagine that the view of the gallows would seduce them to the commission of highway robbery.

A legal provision for the aged, the infirm, and the destitute, is thus unattended with any ill effects. It is also absolutely and imperiously required in every civilised and populous community, by a regard for justice and common humanity. In all such communities the effect of casualties, whether they occur in the order of natural or of political events, is increased in exact proportion to the progress of civilisation and population. An earthquake or an inundation, that unsettles a few cabins or destroys a few individuals in a region inhabited by savage tribes, if it occurs in the territory of a populous nation, sweeps off its thousands, and leaves its tens of thousands destitute of their ordinary means of subsistence. In civilised warfare every battle that is fought deprives a multitude of families of their natural protection. The distress that may be brought upon a populous country by a change in its political condition was sadly proved by the situation of England and many other parts of Europe after the close of the late wars. The events of the last summer in Ireland illustrate the fatal consequences of the casual failure of a crop.

The exposure to such casualties is one of the compensations attending a high state of civilisation and a dense population. It is one of the first and principal duties of the government, in countries thus situated, to guard against such accidents, as far as possible, by the most prudent and careful administration. This, however, on the most favorable supposition, can never be done beyond a certain extent: and it happens unfortunately that these tremendous visitations are much more frequently owing to the faults of rulers than to natural accidents. But from whatever cause they may arise, it would be the height of inhumanity to permit their victims to suffer without relief, or to abandon them to the chance of private charity. The benevolence of individuals will, in all civilised countries, operate in a most favorable manner to supply the deficiencies and obviate the accidental defects of the public institutions of charity. But a wise and efficient organisation of these institutions must form of necessity the basis of every competent system of provision for the poor; and will never be wanting among the political establishments of a generous and Christian country.

The ideas of Mr. Malthus are rather more plausible when applied to institutions intended to relieve the misery resulting directly from private vice. Such, for example, are foundling hospitals, the tenants of which must be supposed in general to be the offspring of illicit connex-

ions.   Such institutions, considered merely in
their effect upon parents, are perhaps in a slight
degree encouragements to vice : although there
is room to suppose that the irregularities in
question can seldom be traced with propriety to
motives of cool calculation.   But in these institutions the child and not the parent is the object
of attention.   An innocent being must not be
deprived of existence, and abandoned to vice
and wretchedness, because it owed its birth to a
fault.   We are not required to visit the sins of
the fathers upon the children ; but we are required to relieve suffering and to preserve life
whenever we can.   Some unfavorable consequences may indirectly result from almost every
act of benevolence ; but for these we are not
responsible : and neither reason nor humanity
authorise us to do evil directly with a view of
avoiding the possible indirect ill effects of doing
good.

   In general, it is one of the least agreeable
consequences of the system of Mr. Malthus, that
it leads of necessity to a low estimate of the
value of life.   Individuals, on the supposition of
its truth, are of no importance.   *Uno avulso non
deficit alter.*   At every vacancy that happens at

the banquet of nature, three or four candidates for the prize are eagerly pushing forward, of whom one only can obtain it. The paragon of animals is of all commodities the cheapest and the most abundant. The loss of a hundred thousand lives is supplied at once, and is of no real importance to the general good. Hence the consequence that life may be expended without remorse to any extent by any statesman or projector, who conscientiously believes that he can thereby effect some ultimate object of a beneficial character. With the physical value of man, the estimate of his moral worth must also fall of course. It can hardly be supposed that a being, whose life is of no consequence, possesses any high moral qualities, or any rights that are entitled to attention. The natural social feeling which leads us to regard such a being with benevolence and respect is a mere deception : and no good reason can be given why the few, who have discovered the secret, should not take advantage of it to promote their own private views at the expense of the interest and happiness of others.

Such, I am sure, are not the sentiments of Mr. Malthus ; but such sentiments are unquestionably the natural effects of his theory. Fortunately the benevolent feelings, as they are not the result of calculation, will never be materially shaken by sophistry. Nevertheless the operation of this system, as far as it is believed and adopted, is to deprive these sentiments of any rational foundation, and to place them in fact in opposition with the dictates of sound sense. The friends of humanity who acquiesce at present in the truth of the principles in question, would therefore probably not regret, as has lately been admitted by one of the most distinguished among them, to find these principles satisfactorily refuted. I venture to hope that the arguments, adduced in the preceding chapters, have shown that they are as much at variance with experience and reason, as they are with common humanity and an elevated notion of the character and destiny of man.

CHAPTER XI.

On the Wages of Labor.

THE wages of labor are its products. Hence
if labor becomes more productive, as population
increases on a given territory, the natural conse
quence would be that the wages of labor must
rise in proportion. As this result does not uniformly happen, it is necessary to examine the
causes which regulate the rate of wages, and
make it vary in many cases from the natural
standard.

If every member of the community enjoyed
the whole fruits of his labor, or the value of them
in money, it is evident that the same cause, that
is, the increase of skill, which makes the labor
of the community more productive as it increases
in population, would also make the labor of
every individual more productive in the same
proportion ; or rather the increased productiveness of the labor of the community is the result
of the increased productiveness of the labor of
all its members. But if the products of the labor

of the community are distributed among its
members upon any other principle than that of
giving to each member the fruits of his own
labor, it is evident that the productiveness of
labor in general will form no certain criterion of
the reward of individual labor, or in other words,
of the rate of wages. The rate of wages will in
this case be a compound result of the productiveness of labor, and of the principles upon
which the products of the labor of the community are distributed among its members.

These principles form every where one of the
most important parts of the political institutions :
and they are essentially different in almost every
different country. In many of the most considerable states of ancient and modern times, the
mass of the population have been considered as
entitled to no share whatever in the fruits of
their own labor. The laborers in this case are
said to be slaves, and wages are wholly unknown.
Although the master is clothed and fed by the
labor of the slave, the slave is supposed to have
no legal right even to the share of its products
necessary for his own subsistence, but is said to
be fed and clothed by the bounty of his master.
In such a situation man loses his moral value,

and is no better than the most intelligent and serviceable of the beasts of burden.

There are other communities in which the right of all the members to the fruits of their own labor is recognised and protected by law, but in which the state of property makes the mass of the population almost absolutely dependent upon a very few individuals. If a populous territory is distributed among a small number of proprietors, so that the mass of the people have little or no opportunity of exercising their industry except for the purpose of supplying the wants or performing the commands of the proprietors, it is obvious that the rate of wages will be very low, whatever may be the productiveness of labor. A society thus constituted, tends of necessity to decay and dissolution. The rewards of labor are insufficient to support the laborer and his family in health and comfort. The population first becomes stationary, and then gradually declines. The country seems to be wasted by a silent but fatal pestilence; and, without any external shock or apparent interior convulsion, it sinks in wealth and power at every successive generation, and finally takes the form of an uncultivated and uninhabited desert. The history of the world is filled with examples of this description. None perhaps is more striking than that of the island of Sicily, which once maintained twelve million inhabitants in abundance, and exported at the same time such quantities of corn as to be called the granary of the Roman empire. Its population is now limited to a few ignorant and barbarous nobles, and a few hundred thousand half-starved and wretched peasants.

The unfavorable effect of such a state of property upon the rate of wages would be augmented, and the decline of the country would be still more rapid, if the magistrates, that represent the community, exacted from the laborer a large part of his earnings under the pretext of paying the necessary expense of protecting him in the enjoyment of his personal rights and the scanty residue of his wages. It has generally happened however, by a sort of compensation, that where the state of property is extremely vicious, the taxes are also comparatively light.

A vicious state of property may however reduce considerably the rewards of individual labor, without entirely checking the progress of population. In this case a principle of improvement will be constantly at work. The number of laborers will be regularly increasing. The productiveness of labor being also increased in the same proportion, all the articles of use and enjoyment will become more abundant. The consumption of them will be extended in consequence, and the whole society will put on an aspect of new activity and wealth. The products of the joint labor of the community, and the wages of individual labor, will both be augmented; although the latter may not be so high as in some other less populous communities where the state of property is more favorable to the importance of individuals. Such has been the progress of events in Great Britain, where the great improvement in the political institutions and in the internal condition of the country, that took place after the close of the civil wars led to an increase of population, to a great extension of labor in all its departments, and to the most remarkable improvements in the modes of its application. The wages of labor rose in proportion to the increase of its productiveness; and when not depressed by accidental causes, are now much higher than they were formerly, though certainly far from being so high as they would be if the fruits of the labor of the whole nation were more equally distributed among its members. The population of England and Wales is about the same with that of the United States of America; but while the total product of the labor of the former countries is far greater than that of the latter, the wages of individual labor with the latter are much higher than with the former; because in the United States (excepting in those parts where the land is cultivated by slaves) every individual enjoys the entire fruits of his own labor, with scarcely any diminution either from the taxes or the state of property.

It may be taken therefore as a general rule, that the population and productiveness of labor being given, the rate of wages will depend upon the circumstances, political and economical, which regulate the distribution of the fruits of the labor of the community among its members.

The differences in the rates of wages, as estimated in money, may not however in all cases correspond precisely with the differences in their real value as computed in the necessaries of life. If we suppose the quantity of money in every country to be fixed, the money value of the necessaries of life will decrease in proportion to their abundance : and, on this supposition, if the necessaries of life are four times as abundant in one country as they are in another, any given sum of money will procure in the former four times as large a supply of the necessaries of life as in the latter. Hence if the nominal rate of wages be one shilling a day in the former, and four in the latter, the real rate in both will be precisely the same. It is true that where every other article of use and enjoyment is abundant, money, considered as a material object, will also abound in the same proportion. The supply of the precious metals, as compared with the demand, will probably be as great as that of corn or cotton ; and as far as the supply of money is augmented, the rise occasioned by it in the nominal value of the necessaries of life will counterbalance the fall occasioned by the abundance of the latter, and keep up the nominal rate of wages. But in reality the demand for a material medium of exchange does not increase in proportion to the increase in the productiveness of labor, and the abundance of its products. Credit is soon found to be a far more convenient instrument for the transaction of business on a considerable scale than money: and the latter is hardly used except for the daily occasions of civil and domestic life.

These considerations serve to account in part for the difference in the nominal rate of wages in England and the United States, which seems at first to be greater than a comparison of the political and personal situation of individuals would naturally lead us to expect.

CHAPTER XII.

Recapitulation.

THE theory maintained in the present work has been stated, for the purpose of brevity, in so very condensed a form, that the essay itself is little more than a summary of the principal heads of the argument; and it may appear unnecessary to attempt a recapitulation of them in a separate chapter. I shall, however, venture to exhibit again the leading points of the discussion in a still more naked shape, in the hope that a review of them may convey to the reader's mind a more accurate notion of the scope of the reasoning, and of the connexion between the several propositions that have been successively supported in the course of the work.

In the first chapter I have stated, as a preliminary objection to the theories of Godwin and Malthus, that they suppose on the one hand, that political institutions are the source of all evil, and on the other, that they have no tendency to improve the condition of mankind, and are entirely indifferent. The former proposition is directly maintained by Godwin, and the latter is implied in the theory of Malthus, which attributes all our miseries to a necessary and permanent excess of population, entirely independent of political institutions. Without attempting to substantiate by argument the value of these institutions, I have taken for granted that it would be admitted by all the persons to whom I wish to address myself : and if it be, the falsehood of the two theories in which it is denied must be conceded of course.

In the second chapter I have advanced the new idea which forms the leading principle of the work, and which is, that the increase of population is a cause of abundance, and not of scarcity ; since it augments the supply of labor in precisely the same proportion with the demand for its products, and developes at the same time the new element of skill, by means of which the same quantity of labor is applied with greater effect, and becomes more productive than before. This proposition is dwelt upon in the second and third chapters, and proved by a reference to general principles and to the history of civilisation. If correct, it shows that the theory of

Malthus is not only false, but directly the reverse of the truth.

But admitting that labor naturally becomes more productive, and the means of subsistence more abundant, in consequence of an increase of population, there will still be a danger of scarcity resulting from this circumstance, wherever the possible supply of the means of subsistence is, or is likely to be, exhausted. The theory of Mr. Malthus supposes that this is permanently the precise state of things in all parts of the world, in consequence of a universal tendency to an excess of population and deficiency of food, arising from the different rates at which food and population naturally increase. It is necessary therefore to refute this objection, in order to establish the theory maintained in the second and third chapters.

This I have attempted to do in the fourth and fifth chapters, by showing, first, that the argument takes for granted that a given population must necessarily subsist upon the direct products of the soil they occupy—a supposition quite groundless in itself, and refuted by a great variety of examples, as for instance that of the city of London: and, secondly, that the rate of increase of the human species, assumed by Mr. Malthus as true, being deduced from a single case, and not from an average of all the known cases, involves a logical error, and in point of fact is a great deal too high. Each of these errors is of itself sufficient to destroy the force of the objection.

The proposition, that the increase of population is a principle of abundance and not of scarcity, being thus established in a positive way, and cleared of the only objection that can be made to it, it becomes unnecessary for the present purpose to ascertain what the rate of increase of the human species really is, and what the causes are that determine the extent of population. But as these are interesting questions, and have generally been discussed in connexion with the inquiry whether the increase of population be a principle of abundance or of scarcity, I have briefly touched upon them in the sixth and seventh chapters, where I have shown that the extent of population is determined almost wholly by the degree of civilisation ; and that its increase is checked at every stage of civilisation by particular forms of moral and physical evil, the operation of which may be indefinitely diminished, but can never be wholly removed, and will always prevent the earth from being overstocked with inhabitants.

This theory is illustrated in the eighth chapter by a reference to the example of the United States of America. The unprecedented increase of population in that country is attributed to its extraordinary political and geographical situation, by means of which the inhabitants have been almost wholly exempt from the influence of the checks on population that have generally existed in communities at the same point of civilisation. It is attributed, in other words, to the goodness of the social institutions and the good morals of the people. The abundance of the means of subsistence enjoyed there is stated to be the consequence and not the cause of their favorable moral and political situation; and this point is illustrated by a reference to the case of the neighboring Indians, whose position is precisely the same in every particular excepting that of civilisation, and who, instead of increasing in population and living in abundance, are diminishing in numbers and dying of want.

These three chapters, though they illustrate the subject, have no immediate connexion with the main argument of the essay.

The proposition, that the increase of population is a principle of abundance and not of scarcity, being established, and the opposite theory of Mr. Malthus refuted, the conclusions which he has drawn from this theory, of the propriety of discouraging marriage and abolishing the poor laws, fall of themselves. I have briefly stated this point in the ninth and tenth chapters, and have taken the occasion to remark, that the inconsistency between the system of this writer and the benevolent and social instincts of our nature, which lead to the universal prevalence of early marriages, and to the establishment of institutions for the relief of the destitute, furnishes, independently of any more positive objection, a strong presumption of its falsehood.

In the eleventh chapter I have explained the manner in which the state of civilisation affects the rate of wages, and prevents in many cases the rewards of individual labor from increasing in proportion to the increased productiveness of the labor of the community.

Such are the principal points which have been successively touched upon in the preceding work. The leading propositions which I have maintained certainly present themselves to my mind with a high degree of evidence ; and, as far as I am acquainted with the subject, are entirely new. Whether they will appear to the public either new or important, I can hardly undertake to anticipate. However this may be, I shall not regret that I have devoted a few pages to a defence of social and benevolent feelings, should it even prove to have been conducted on false principles : and I flatter myself that the work, though controversial in its nature, will not tend by its manner to excite malignant passion ; but rather to encourage the same kind sentiments which it was written to defend.

THE END.

THE

UNITED STATES MAGAZINE,

AND

DEMOCRATIC REVIEW.

VOL. XVII.

OCTOBER, 1845.

No. LXXXVIII.

THE MALTHUSIAN THEORY.

DISCUSSED IN A CORRRRESPONDENCE BETWEEN ALEX. H. EVERETT, AND PROF. GEO. TUCKER, OF THE UNIVERSITY OF VIRGINIA.*

NO. I.

Mr. Everett to Prof. Tucker.

Washington, D. C., April 23, 1844.

DEAR SIR,—In several passages of your late very able and interesting address to the National Institute, you assumed, as an ascertained principle of political economy, that the rate of wages regularly declines with the increasing density of population.

In my work entitled, " New Ideas on Population, with remarks on the theories of Godwin and Malthus," I endeavor to prove that the rate of wages regularly rises with the increasing density of population.

As the principle in question is a very important one, I am deirous to have the benefit of your deliberate opinion upon it. Although you mentioned to me in conversation that you had read the work just alluded to, I thought it possible that the subject might not have particularly attracted your attention, and it was with the view of bringing it distinctly to your notice that I took the liberty of saying to you that I would write you a short letter upon it.

I will not trouble you by recapitulating here the argument in favor of my opinion, which you will find in my book. I should be happy to hear from you on the subject, and to furnish, if you desire it, any explanations that may be in my possession. My address is at Boston.

With great respect, I am, dear sir, very truly your friend, and obedient serv't.

Signed,   A. H. EVERETT.

Hon. George Tucker.

---

* Having known a few months ago that a correspondence was in progress between Mr. Alexander H. Everett, now our Minister to China, and Professor Tucker, of the University of Virginia, on the important and interesting subject of the Doctrine of Population and Wages, on which those two distinguished and accomplished gentlemen held different opinions—Mr. Everett being strongly anti-Malthusian, and Professor Tucker, to a great extent, if not entirely, Malthusian—we suggested to one of the two gentlemen that it would be an useful mode of spreading before the public the materials for an enlightened judgment on this much vexed question, to publish the correspondence. The ready assent of both to this request having been obtained, the result is the appearance of the present pages. The present publication contains an argument on each side. Two replies and corresponding rejoinders, have since taken place—Professor Tucker in each case leading off in the amicable and courteous encounter of opinions, and being followed by Mr. Everett. The last letter from the latter gentleman is dated from on board the U. S. ship-of-the-line Columbus, being written during the passage of that vessel from New York to Rio de Janeiro, on the way to China. The two friendly combatants being now at the antipodes of the globe in reference to each other, the correspondence on this subject may now therefore be said to have reached its termination. According to the natural division into *pairs of letters,* we divide it into three parts, which will be given in three of our successive numbers. Without note or comment by ourselves, (though strongly anti-Malthusian, of course, in our economical philosophy,) we shall leave every reader to judge for himself to which side of the argument the preponderance of truth inclines. Whichever of the two able and eminent gentlemen may be deemed to have stood enlisted on the side of the weaker cause, none will question, at least, his right to the full application of the line—

——*Si Pergama dextra*
Defendi possent, etiam hac defensa fuissent.

NO. II.

Professor Tucker to Mr. Everett.

University of Virginia, May 14, 1844.

MY DEAR SIR,—When your letter from Washington reached me I chanced to be engaged in preparing some sheets for the press, and I thought it better to delay my answer until I could give an undivided attention to the subject, which, I agree with you, is an important one, and which would seem from the opposite views entertained of it, to be also one of difficulty.

I do not wonder at your dissent from the theory of Malthus. When I first read his book, it appeared to me to afford so dangerous an apology for bad government, and to present so cheerless a view of human society, that I revolted at it, and felt assured that it was founded on fallacies, which it would not be difficult to detect, and I accordingly, some years afterwards, attempted an answer to it, which was one of a series of Essays published in Washington in 1822, though written eight or ten years before. I then endeavored to show that the tendency of mankind to increase was over-rated by Mr. Malthus ; " that when the natural course of things is not disturbed by the mistakes of government, or the errors of national opinion, numbers will not reach a dangerous or mischievous excess;" that " the stock of human happiness is likely to increase with the increase of numbers;" with other propositions contravening his theory. I have since read much, and thought much, on the subject, and have persuaded myself that while Malthus's premises are in the main true, it is quite as reasonable to say that since man is exposed to so many evils, physical and moral, which are destructive of life, and which he cannot evade or subdue, his multiplying propensity is necessary to counteract them, as to say that vice and misery, (in default of moral restraint,) are necessary to check the undue force of that propensity. Such, accordingly, has been the ground that I have always taken in my lectures on Political Economy, in this institution.

You see then, sir, that we do not differ in our general opinion of this celebrated theory as to the melancholy consequences, which it considers to be the inevitable result of man's tendency to increase and multiply. But it seems that we do differ on the effect of that increase on the wages of labor. Instead of " wages regularly rising with the increasing density of population," as you maintain, I have come to the conclusion that the general and natural, but not inevitable tendency of such increasing tendency is to lower wages, and that the occasional exceptions to the general rule are but temporary.

To narrow the field of discussion, I will state the general principles on which I rely. If these postulates be conceded by you,—as I think they will,—then we can differ only about the inferences. If, however, any one or more of them be denied, it is unnecessary to proceed farther, until our disagreement about them is adjusted. They are—

1. That all human subsistence is derived from the earth, principally from the products of the soil, or the animals nourished by them, and in a very small proportion from the products of the waters.

2. That the quantity of food thus furnished has natural limits, which cannot be exceeded, whether it be equal to the support of 200 to the square mile, or of twice or thrice that number.

3. That man, in common with other animals, has the power and the propensity of multiplication, so that if this propensity has not strong counteractions, such as want of food, disease, &c., population will double in a given time.

4. That when it is uninfluenced by these considerations, the faculty of doubling (comprehending both the capacity and inclination) is in every stage of its progressive increase, as great or nearly as great as it was at first.

5. That the quantity of human aliment which any portion of the earth can produce, until its utmost limit is reached, is in proportion to its fertility and the degree of human industry and skill exerted on it.

6. That the number of persons which can be supported on a given area is dependent partly on the quantity it can produce, and partly on the character of the aliment; the same area being capable of producing generally less animal than vegetable food, and less of some kinds of vegetable food than of others.

7. That the means of subsistence are unequally distributed among the members of the same community ; so that while some have an ample supply, others may not have enough for comfort, or even to support life.

From these general facts and laws it follows that in an isolated community, if the population increase, it must be either because the soil is made to produce more food, of the same character and in the same proportion as it previously produced, or that the average food consumed by each individual is less in quantity or inferior in quality. When the sharers are more in number, either the sum to be shared must be augmented, or each one's dividend must be diminished. In the first case the laborer receives the same return for his labor ; in the last, he receives less.

But it must be recollected that food cannot go on increasing ; and whether the soil be capable of supporting 100 or 500 to the square mile, that limit will be reached after a few periods of duplication. Thus, suppose the population to be only ten to the square mile, which is less than the average in the settled parts of the United States, then in the first period of duplication the numbers would be 20 to the square mile : in the

2d	.	.	. 40
3d	.	.	. 80
4th	.	.	160
5th	.	.	. 320
6th	.	.	. 640

which last is a degree of density which we may consider to be physically impossible, since the acre which would be here required to maintain an individual must furnish him not only with food, but with clothing, fuel, and all the other comforts of life derived from the natural world.

In this progress of population every increase of numbers makes a corresponding increase of food necessary. But after the whole land of a country is taken into cultivation, the increase of its product is more and more difficult. It may be easy enough to raise that product from five bushels per acre to ten, and even from ten to twenty. But to raise it from 20 to 40 would be a slower process, and one requiring a far greater expense of labor and capital ; and then to double that product might be physically impossible ; or if not, it certainly would be to raise it from 80 bushels to 160 per acre. Yet in all these stages the tendency to multiply may be as strong as it was at first ; and the increase of population is adjusted to the dimishing rate of increase of food by the smaller amount of raw produce allotted to the laborer—in other words, by lower wages.

Perhaps it will be said that prudence naturally checks this multiplying propensity ; and that men marrying only when they are able to support a family, the increase of numbers will go on *pari passu* with the increase of food. If the amount consumed by each individual were a constant quantity, then I admit that the increase of population could not exceed that of the products of the soil. But this amount is a varying quantity, admitting of great contraction. The human stomach does indeed require to be filled, as Adam Smith remarks ; but it makes a great difference as to the number which a given surface will support, whether it be filled with meat or bread, and yet more with bread or potatoes. Now experience shows that when population is up to the level of the means of liberal subsistence, the generative faculty still rules ; and forcing a greater number into existence, the excess are compelled to put up with a cheaper mode of subsistence ;—to substitute, to a greater or less extent, vegetable food for animal, and potatoes or other roots for bread. And inasmuch as the rich consume as liberally as before, the whole of the necessary reduction falls upon the poor, that is, the laboring class, who have thus to take yet less raw produce for their labor or lower wages.

Does observation confirm these speculative views? It does. Thus, according to a comparative estimate made some years since on authentic facts, the quantity of food earned per week, in India, England and the United States was as follows :

In India, 20 2-5 cwt. parts of rice.

" England, 80 wheat.

" U. States, 192 wheat.

The rate of wages, too, varies in the different parts of this country, if estimated in raw produce, and decreases with density of numbers. Thus :

In the New England States the average rate is 2 pecks per day.

Middle States, 3¼ pecks per day.

Western States, 3 9.00   "

We have evidence also, that real wages have fallen in England with the increase of population, though, for reasons to be hereafter noticed, the fall of the one has not been in proportion to the increase of the other. The ordinary wages of day labour has lately been a peck of wheat, or something less a day, and it is stated to have been some centuries since two pecks a day, though I cannot now recall the authority for the fact. But, by a table published by Arthur Young, and to be found in Lowe's Appendix, the price of labor from the early part of the 18th century to the beginning of the 19th, had risen from 10 to 20, while wheat had risen in the same period from $7\frac{3}{4}$ to 20,—thus showing that, estimating the laborer's wages in wheat, they had risen more than 25 per cent., or more accurately as $7\frac{3}{4}$ to 20. And Barton, in his work " on the state of the laboring classes," details the rate of wages in wheat, from about 1747 to 1807,— and he estimates the decline in 60 years to be from 102 pints of wheat per week to 60 pints.

The inherent difficulty, not to say impossibility, of wages continuing to rise with the increasing density of population, may be farther shown by the following illustration. Let us suppose a country dependent on its own resources, (for to such my attention is now confined) with a population of forty persons to the square mile—about the present population of Ohio. This allows to each inhabitant, on an average, the product of 16 acres. When the population shall have doubled, or reached 80 to the square mile, that allows to each one the product of 8 acres. The next duplication would of course limit the average consumption to the product of 4 acres, and if we suppose it to attain 320 to the square mile, which is less than the present population of England, exclusive of Wales, that density would reduce the quota to 2 acres. Now it would be conceding a great deal to admit that, by any improvement in husbandry, first 8 acres, then 4, and finally but 2, could be made to yield as much as the 16 had done,—especially when for some articles consumed by men, such as timber and fuel, (if the country contained no fossil coal or peat) the product can be but moderately increased by human in-

dustry and skill. But if this liberal concession, warranted by no experience, be made, it would suppose the wages of labor to be merely undiminished but not increased. To infer such increase, we must suppose that the reduced number of acres has *actually produced more* than the larger number, so that not only half the land is made to yield more than the whole had done, but the fourth more than either, and the eighth the most of all. When we recollect how extremely difficult it is only to quadruple the product of poor land, and that it is impossible so to multiply that of the rich land, and not easy even to double it, the greatest average increase on all the lands, which has been here supposed, and which is the undisguisable condition of an increase of wages, seems to be utterly inadmissible, even on this simple *à priori* view of the subject. Such a result, too, is rendered yet more marvellous and incredible by the fact, that when the general average of the land to each individual is reduced from 16 acres to 2, a portion of the society still retains much more than their proportionate part,— some even the original 16 acres,—for their exclusive consumption in pleasure grounds, preserves of game, forests, &c. So that we must conclude that as population advances to density, and each individual must subsist on a smaller portion of the earth's surface—the increased subsistence required is met, partly by making the soil more productive, and partly by the great body of the community,—comprehending the laboring class, *consuming cheaper and coarser food.* And since that class obtain but the means of subsistence for their labor—at least in densely peopled countries—to say that their subsistence deteriorates with increasing numbers, is the same as saying that wages fall.

Both Malthus and Ricordo agree that raw produce rises with the progress of population, and this is virtually admitting that labor falls: for raw produce rises only by its exchanging for greater quantities of labor. Ricordo, indeed, paradoxically as I think, maintains that labor rises as well as raw produce ; but even he admits that the laborer will receive, in the progress of society, a smaller amount of raw produce, and that not only his command of corn, but his general condition will be deteriorated. Though Adam Smith does not formally notice the effect of an increase of population on wages, he virtually recognises the principles here insisted on by adverting to and explaining the facts that the real wages of labor (which he defines to be the amount of the necessaries and conveniences of life received by the laborer) are higher in this country than in England, and are at the lowest point of depression in the crowded population of China.

Thus, you see, sir, that I am able to adduce fact, reasoning, and authority in support of the opinion I advanced that wages naturally fall with the progress of population.

I have hitherto been considering a community isolated from the rest of the world, or rather supported directly from its soil; which, indeed, I think, is the best way of ascertaining the proper effect and influence of an increase of population on wages. But as you rely, in support of your views, upon the ability of a thriving, prosperous nation, to draw supplies of raw produce from abroad in exchange for products of its skill and industry, I readily admit that this is practicable under particular circumstances, and that, by this means, wages, not merely nominal but real, may increase with increasing numbers. Such a nation may derive a part of its supplies from countries newly settled, and consequently underpeopled, like the United States and New Holland;—or from such countries as Poland, which, having no manufactures, are willing to give a part of their raw produce in exchange for them. This has, for half a century or more, been the condition of Great Britain, who has regularly, during that period, drawn part of her subsistence from other countries, especially Ireland. But besides that even here this counteraction to the general law I have insisted on has not been sufficient to *arrest* the decline of wages, but only to check it, *such counteraction cannot be permanent.* In the same degree that one country produces less than it consumes, the others from which she draws her supplies, must produce more; and as her demands increase with her increasing population, so must their excess. But that, we have seen, is physically impossible. So that when they have reached the limit of their utmost supply, the law, apportioning wages to population, which had been

suspended or checked, is immediately renewed in full force. Besides, the strong tendency which mankind have ever shown to increase to the level of subsistence, may be supposed to be constantly operating in the countries affording the supply, and, sooner or later, to consume all that they raise. That result may be confidently expected in the United States; and, at a reduced rate of increase, they are not likely, in a century more, to have any surplus provisions for export. Even in Poland, where the nobles are too proud to engage in manufactures, and the serfs too poor and too ignorant, a farther increase of numbers would have been likely to make them turn a part of their labor to manufactures, necessity and want having been the great parents of invention. Since they have exchanged their absurd government for another, they will probably increase with the rest of the Russian, Prussian, and Austrian dominions, and, in time, have no regular surplus of grain.

I do not think that any argument can be drawn from the supplies which great cities, like London, draw from the country. As a half or even a third of the population are sufficient to raise raw produce for the rest, and as the other operations of industry are better carried on in towns, the people of every country naturally distribute themselves into two portions, one in the country and the other in towns, but whether in many small ones or a few large ones, depends on the rivers, harbours, and other localities, and on their commerce and manufactures. The progress of population tends to enlarge these cities, but, as we have seen, to lessen the supplies that can be exported, and, consequently, that can be imported.

I have thus far considered the *raw produce* earned by the laborer as the *measure of his wages*, because it is the most indispensable, and constitutes the largest part of his expense. But your position, that labour becomes more productive as it increases in quantity, is entirely correct as to manufactures, and all the other comforts of life, except food. By means of the division of labor and the steady progress of inventive art and productive skill, our clothes, furniture, utensils of all sorts, are constantly becoming cheaper and better. Indeed, this result is partly produced by the greater cheapness of human labor, in consequence of its multiplication, of which I have spoken :—and it is probable that it was because your attention was too exclusively drawn to this striking effect of a dense population, and to the particular circumstances of the United States, where labor is more and more productive, that you have been led to your general theory.

The circumstances of the United States are, however, peculiar. Here a people possessing the arts and the husbandry of a dense population, are in possession of a vacant, or almost vacant, territory, and, of course, there is nothing to lessen the wages of labour, when measured in raw produce, until the whole country is settled and its best lands taken into cultivation,—while their increase of population is constantly adding to the productiveness of their labor in every other employment.

Nor have the wages of labor fallen in England, at all in proportion to the increase of its population, in the last half century. But her situation has also some peculiarities. Her vast colonial possessions, her extensive foreign commerce, her abundance of coal and iron, by which she has been able to profit so immensely by the inventions of Watt, Arkwright, &c., have enabled her to buy the grain of Ireland, (and of other countries whenever she wanted it,) to supply her own deficiency. Her husbandry has, moroever, been greatly improved of late years, and vast tracts of commons, before worthless, have been added to her arable lands, so that the increase of her agricultural produce has almost kept pace with the increase of her population. These checks, however, to the law which regulates wages, are but temporary ; and if her population continues to increase, the wages of her laborers, in conformity to that law, must decline.

You have in favor of your views, the concurrence of Gray, in his work on the "Happiness of States,"—of Lowe, in his "State of England," and of some other English writers of respectability. But after reading all they have written on the subject, I find nothing in their books which you have not substantially stated, and consequently consider that the answers which I have given to your views are equally applicable to theirs.

Perhaps you will ask, if I agree with Malthus as to the increased difficulty experienced by the laborer in earning subsistence in an increasing population, in what do I differ from him. My answer is, that I differ from him as to the force of the preventive checks, which I think that Malthus has underrated,—that in this country especially, where we start with a higher standard of comfort to the common laborer than exists elsewhere, or probably ever has existed in any extensive country, it is not improbable that prudent forbearance of marriage until the means of ordinary comfort can be attained, will operate sooner and more forcibly than it seems to have done generally in the old world ;—and lastly, that when population has reached its utmost density, consistent with the general comfort of the people, by reason of the large proportion of the population, that will then be found in cities, which cannot keep up their supply of inhabitants without recruits from the country, and of a moderate retardation of marriage, the annual supply of life will not exceed its annual waste, and, consequently, there will not exist that pressure of population on the means of subsistence, supposed by Mr. Malthus, or the sufferings it occasions.

At the risk of being tedious, I have thus fully detailed my views on this interesting subject, and though I dare not venture to hope that I shall make you a convert to my opinions, having seldom had that good fortune in my discussion of speculative topics, I thought I would at least satisfy you that the doctrine I advanced had been the result of much thought and deliberation, and was supported by not a few arguments, such as they are. It will give me pleasure to learn from you the points on which we may still differ.

I am, very respectfully and sincerely, your friend.

(Signed,)   GEORGE TUCKER.
Hon. A. H. Everett, Boston.

NO. III.

Mr. Everett to Professor Tucker.

New York, May 29, 1844.

DEAR SIR,—I received here yesterday your friendly and interesting letter of the 14th inst. I feel myself greatly obliged by the attention which you had given to my request, and by the careful manner in which you have answered it.

I am staying here a few days, on a visit to some personal friends, and shall return next week to Massachusetts, where I shall have more leisure to reflect upon the subject. After deliberately weighing your suggestions with the respect to which they are, on all accounts, so fully entitled, I will take the liberty of troubling you with some further observations upon the points on which we differ.

I am, dear sir, very truly and respectfully, your friend,

(Signed,)   A. H. EVERETT.

Hon. George Tucker.

NO. IV.

Mr. Everett to Professor Tucker.

Washington, D. C., Jan. 29, 1845.

DEAR SIR,—I have deferred answering your very interesting letter of the 14th of May last, until I should have had time to give the subject of it a full consideration, and to review my opinions upon it in connnection with your suggestions. I will now, agreeably to your desire, state to you as concisely as I can, my views of the points upon which we differ.

In your Address to the Institute, you assumed, as an ascertained principle in Political Economy, that the reward of labor, or, in the common phrase, the rate of wages regularly declines with the progress of population. I took the liberty to request from you an explanation of the grounds upon which you assumed this principle as true, and stated as my opinion that the rate of wages regularly rises, or, in other words, that labor regularly becomes more productive, as population increases in density.

In your letter now before me, you say that my position is " entirely correct as to manufactures and all the other comforts of life, excepting food : that by means of the division of labor, and the steady progress of the inventive arts and of practical skill, our clothes, furniture, and utensils of all sorts, are also becoming cheaper and better." You also agree that the progress of population increases the productiveness of agricultural labor ; but you think that this increase is less rapid than in the case of labor employed in manufactures, and that there is a limit beyond which the amount of the produce of a given tract of land cannot possibly be carried.

On all these points we entirely concur. I now come to those upon which we differ. You maintain that population naturally increases everywhere, with great rapidity, excepting so far as it is kept in check by a deficiency in the supply of provisions, and that the inhabitants of every part of the globe must necessarily subsist upon the produce of the territory which they occupy. These positions being admitted, it would, as you say, follow of course, that a given amount of produce must be distributed everywhere among a constantly increasing number of persons, and that each will receive a smaller share : in other words, that, as population advances, the reward of labor will be diminished, or, in technical phrase, the rate of wages will decline.

I differ from you in regard to the correctness of both these positions. On a review of the past and contemporary state of the world, I see no reason to believe that population, under ordinary circumstances, naturally increases with great rapidity, or that the population of every part of the globe must necessarily subsist upon the produce of the soil they occupy. I am satisfied, on the contrary, that a rapid increase of population,—or indeed any increase at all,—is a comparatively rare occurrence, indicating, wherever it takes place, an uncommonly prosperous condition of the society :—that such an increase naturally brings with it an increase in the productiveness of labor in all its departments, less rapid, no doubt, in agriculture than in manufactures, but capable in both of being carried to an indefinite extent ;—and that, although the amount of the means of subsistence, which can be drawn from a given territory, is limited by its extent, the amount at the disposal of the inhabitants is not limited by that or any other cause, but may be raised by importation to any quantity, which the demand may require. The increase in the amount of the supplies, both of agriculture and manufactured articles, occasioned by an increase of population, being thus more than proportional to the increased number of consumers, it follows, of necessity, that unless there be some artificial inequality in the mode of distribution, each person will receive a larger share than he did before ;—in other words, that the reward of labor, or rate of wages, will rise.

In order to simplify the discussion, and keep it within a moderate compass, I will waive, for the present, any examination of the supposed tendency to a rapid increase of population, and confine myself to a few remarks on your second position, namely, that the quantity of provisions at the disposal of a community is necessarily limited to the direct product of the soil they occupy. If it can be shown, on the contrary, that the amount of produce, whether manufactured or agricultural, at the disposal of a community, is limited only by the extent of the demand, and that an increase of population, whenever it occurs, is a principle of abundance and not of scarcity,—it will, of course, follow that there can be no decline of wages resulting from this cause, at least until the whole productive power of the globe shall be exhausted,—a contingency which, for the present purpose, may be safely left out of view.

In order to bring the question to a point, let us suppose a community occupying a territory where the limit of the possible amount of agricultural produce has been reached ; and let us suppose the population of this community to be doubled. As there is no further employment for agricultural labor, the additional members of the community will, of course, engage in the various branches of manufactures ; and on the principle, in which we agree, that the progress of population increases very rapidly and to an indefinite extent the productiveness of the labor employed in manufactures, this whole class of products (including, according to your enumeration, clothes, furniture, and all sorts of machinery) is consequently much cheaper, as compared with any fixed standard of value, than it was before. The productiveness of agricultural labor not having increased at all, its products remain of the same value, in comparison with any fixed standard, and are, of course, dearer in exchange with manufactures. If a barrel of flour would before exchange for a yard of broad-cloth, it will now exchange for two. In the mean time

the rate of exchange between flour and broad-cloth remains the same as before in other countries where no increase of population has taken place. In France and England a barrel of flour exchanges for two yards of broadcloth ; in Poland it still exchanges for only one. The merchants, whose business it is to watch the markets and take advantage of differences of this kind in the value of the same articles in different places, now purchase cloth in England or France, exchange it in Poland at the rate of a yard to the barrel, carry their flour to London or Paris, where they sell it at the rate of two yards to the barrel, and thus realize upon the operation a profit of one hundred per cent. deducting charges, whatever they may be. But in every branch of business which yields a profit beyond the usual rate, competition, of course, springs up immediately. Other merchants engage in the trade, and content themselves with smaller gains, until the profit is reduced to the ordinary rate. A barrel of flour now sells in England for a sum sufficient to reward, at the ordinary rate, all the labor that has been employed in bringing it to market. Now the labor employed in bringing a barrel of Polish flour to London is, in this case, the labor employed upon a yard of British cloth, and that employed by the merchant in transporting the cloth to Poland and the flour to London. If cloth has fallen 100 per cent. at London in consequence of the increase of population, flour must also fall 100 per cent, excepting so far as the price may be increased by the freight and charges incurred in the two voyages.

What then will be the reward of labor or rate of wages at London, compared with what it was before the increase of population took place? Estimated in manufactures, it has risen 100 per cent. Estimated in agricultural produce, and allowing 50 per cent. for freight and charges on the two voyages, it has risen 50 per cent. If these two classes of products be supposed to enter in equal parts into the consumption of the community, the average rise will, of course, be a medium between the two rates. If wages were before at the rate of a dollar a day, they will now, after the population has been doubled, be $ 1.75. If, as you suppose, although I do not agree with you in this, the rate of wages is regulated exclusively by the state of the supply of agricultural produce, there is still a rise of 50 per cent. A day's labor, which commanded, before the increase of population, only a dollar, now commands, even on this supposition, $1.50.

If, under the same circumstances, we suppose the population to be tripled or quadrupled, there will be, for the same reasons, a proportional increase in the productiveness of labor and in the rate of wages.

The result here contemplated is, as you perceive, the necessary consequence of the regular course of trade, as it proceeds from day to day before our eyes in every part of the world, excepting so far as it is interfered with by the arbitrary regulations of different countries. The theory is verified, at this moment, in large sections of our own country. New England, and even Western New York, receive their means of subsistence, to a considerable extent, from the western states ; and should they continue to increase in population as they have done, must draw still more largely upon the same rich granary.

I will now advert to the objections made in your letter to the possibility or probability of the result here supposed.

After remarking that the inhabitants of a densely peopled country may temporarily obtain a part of their supplies from abroad, you say that " this state of things cannot be permanent. In the same degree that one country produces less than it consumes, the others, from which she draws her supplies, must produce more : and as her demands increase with her increasing population, so must their excess. But this, we have seen, is physically impossible, so that when they have reached the limit of their utmost supply, the law apportioning wages to population, which had been temporarily suspended or checked, is immediately renewed in full force."

In other words, and to continue the illustration employed before :—if the density of population, and with it the demand for foreign grain, should continue to increase in England, the merchant, who has been in the habit of supplying the British market with grain from Poland, would find, after a while, that he had exhausted that field, and that he could no longer carry on with

advantage his former trade between London and Dantzic. What would be the consequence ? Would the corn-merchant discontinue his business because he could no longer freight his ships at the same ports as before ? Of course not, He would now send them to the Black Sea, to the United States, or to any other part of the globe, where grain or flour were to be had. As long as there was an effectual demand for further supplies of grain at London, the corn trade would afford a profit ; and as long as it afforded a profit, it would be carried on with one part of the world or another. The only assignable limit to the extent of the supplies of food that might, if wanted, be obtained in this way, is that of the productive power of the whole globe. When the productive power of the whole globe, land and water, shall have been put in requisition to its utmost extent, if population should still continue to increase, there would, of course, be a deficiency of food. Until the occurrence of such a state of things, which is obviously chimerical, and is admitted to be so by Mr. Malthus and his partisans, there can be no necessary deficiency in any quarter ; and the value of labor, whether estimated in food or any other article, will increase, instead of declining, exactly in proportion as population increases in density.

I have thus, my dear sir, given you my views upon the theory of this subject, as treated in your letter ; and particularly upon the two points stated above, in which we differ. The final test of truth in regard to this or any other theory, is an appeal to facts. You give in confirmation of your views a table of the rates of wages in different countries, in which they are stated at 20 and two-fifths pints of rice per week in India, 80 pints of wheat in England, and 192 pints of wheat in the United States. Of these countries the United States are the one in which population is now increasing with the greatest rapidity ; England probably holds the second place in this respect ; while India is a ruined and exhausted country, in which wealth and population have long been declining, and which is gradually sinking into complete desolation. That the country where population is most rapidly increasing is also the one where the wages of labor are highest ; and that in the country which holds the second place in this respect, they are four times as high as in another where population is declining, are facts which it is not very easy to reconcile with the supposition that an increase of population regularly occasions a comparative scarcity. They coincide very well with any doctrine that an increase of population produces abundance. The same may be said of your statement that in our western country, where population increases more rapidly than in any other part of the Union, the rate of wages, estimated in grain, is nearly four pecks a day; while in the middle states, where population increases somewhat less rapidly, it is only three and a quarter; and in New England, where the increase is still less rapid, only two. It seems to me that each of these cases, if not absolutely fatal to your theory, must be accounted for as an exception to the general rule, and can give it, of course, no direct support.

It is true that, if the rate of wages were affected by no other circumstance except the comparative density of population, it should be, on any view of the subject, higher in England than it is in this country, and higher in New England than it is in the middle and western states. But no one supposes that the state of population is the only circumstance which affects the rate of wages. The state of population determines the productiveness of labor, the products of which are naturally distributed among the members of the community on the principle that every one shall receive the whole produce of his own industry, or its equivalent in money: and so far as this principle is permitted to operate, the rate of wages will be directly proportional to the density of the population. But the operation of this principle is controlled by the political institutions of every country, and in most cases, to a greater or less extent, counteracted; so that the rate of wages is a compound result of the state of population and the character of the government. If, for example, the density of population be twice as great in France as it is in Spain, the rate of wages in the former country would be naturally twice as high as in the latter: but if the French government regularly employ one half of the working men in the army, and half the

produce of the labor of the other moiety in paying the expenses of the wars in which they are engaged, there will remain only one quarter of the regular produce of the labor of the whole population to be distributed among the actual laborers. The rate of wages, instead of being twice as high as it is in Spain, would be only half as high; and so of other cases of a similar kind.

It might appear, at first thought, as if the physical advantages of different countries would have a good deal of weight in determining the reward of individual labor; and that this would naturally be much greater in a very fertile region than it is in a barren one. Such, however, does not seem to be the case: and this is one of the strongest proofs of the ascendancy of the moral part of our nature over the material. All experience shows that the influence of a fine climate and a very productive soil in removing the necessity and with it the disposition to labor, neutralizes entirely the effect that would result from the greater advantages under which labor is applied under such circumstances, and that the total produce is not so great in these countries as it is in those where subsistence is less easy. The inhabitants of the temperate zone, taking the world round, furnish at the year's end a much larger amount of products than those who live within the tropics. The principal economical result of great physical advantages is to cheapen the particular articles that are most favored by the soil and climate, and become, in consequence, the great objects of attention. By estimating the reward of labor in these, it may be made to appear in almost every country much higher than it is in others. Thus the rate of wages, estimated in wine, would appear to be much higher in France than it is in Great Britain or the United States. Estimated in bananas and oranges, it would be higher in the West Indian Islands than in any other part of Christendom. If rice were the standard, labor would be better paid in China and India than in Europe; and if wheat be employed for this purpose, it appears greater in the grain-growing countries than it really is. This is one of the reasons why the rate of wages, estimated in wheat according to your statement, appears so much higher in the United States than in England, instead of being, as it naturally should be, lower ; and is probably the only reason why it appears higher in the western than in the middle and eastern states of this Union. In comparing the reward of labor at different periods in the same country, a particular product of the country, like wheat, is a better test than money ; though still an uncertain one. But in comparing the reward of labor at the same period in different countries, any one article is obviously of little or no value. The only sure test is the general condition of the laborer, that is, of the community at large ; the extent to which the people are supplied with the necessaries, comforts, and luxuries of life ; such as lodging, clothing, fire, food, machinery of all kinds, professional aid, education, religious instruction, and amusements of all descriptions. On applying this test, it will be found, I imagine, that the reward of labor at this and every other period, and in all parts of the world, bears a direct proportion to the density of population, excepting so far as this result is counteracted by political causes, which can generally be distinctly seen and pointed out.

England is precisely the country in which the effect that I ascribe to the increase of population in augmenting the productiveness of labor is most apparent. The reason is that a more than usually large proportional amount has been applied to manufactures, in which there is more room for the improvement of methods, and consequent increase of productiveness than in agriculture. It is calculated that the machinery of all kinds now in use in Great Britain represents the labor of three hundred—some say eight hundred— millions of men. Assuming the former estimate as an approximation to the truth, it follows that the productiveness of labor and the total amount of its products have been augmented, chiefly since the commencement of the present century, 3000 per cent., and that the British nation have at their disposal the means of commanding the labor (or its equivalent in machinery) of three hundred millions of men in other parts of the globe. As the labor of one man employed in agriculture under tolerably favorable circumstances will furnish the means of subsistence for at least

three, it follows that the British nation have at their disposal the means of commanding annually agricultural produce sufficient for the subsistence of the whole human race. Excepting so far as their own arbitrary regulations prevent it, the natural operation of the laws of trade would regularly supply them in their own ports with all the foreign grain that might be wanted, at the low prices at which it is sold in the grain-growing countries, with the addition of the regular charge for transportation, calculated at the lowest possible rate.

From these considerations, which are obvious and undisputed, it results that, whatever may be the reasons which prevent the reward of individual labor in England from being as high as it naturally should be, they are not to be found, as you suppose, in any deficiency in the supply of the means of subsistence. It is unnecessary for the present purpose, and would carry me far beyond the limits of a letter, to go into the inquiry what these reasons are. The large deductions made by the government from the annual produce of the labor of the country to cover the public expenses and pay the interest on the debt (amounting annually to about three hundred million dollars) are undoubtedly one. The Corn Laws are another. A third is probably to be found in the rapidity with which the immense mass of machinery now in use has been introduced, and which has probably not permitted the increased consumption resulting from the greater cheapness of the articles made by machinery to keep pace fully with the increased supply, so as to continue in employment the same number of men as before. Numbers must have been discharged : and as the local situation of England renders it difficult for many of them to find employment elsewhere, the labor market is overstocked, paupers abound, and those who work are obliged to take such wages as they can get. If in a working population of about ten millions, machinery is suddenly introduced, equivalent to the labor of three hundred millions ; in other words, if every working man is suddenly enabled to do the work of thirty, supposing the demand for the products of labor to remain about the same, twenty-nine out of every thirty working men will be thrown out of employment. If the demand and consequent production be doubled by the increased cheapness of the manufactured articles, the labor of two men supplies them, and twenty-eight must still be dismissed. If demand and consumption be ten times greater than before, twenty laborers out of every thirty are, nevertheless, compelled to quit their places ; and so of any other proportion. If the whole ten millions were kept in employment, the result would be equivalent to the labor of three thousand millions of men. However great may have been the increase in the total amount of the produce of British labor, occasioned by the introduction of machinery, it has, of course, remained far below this point. Without claiming any thing like strict accuracy for these estimates, which are merely approximative and of the lowest kind, I incline to think that the sudden introduction of this immense amount of machinery has contributed to a greater extent than is generally supposed to the pauperism, distress, and lowness of wages, that are now combined in England with a profusion of national wealth unparalleled in the history of the world. So far as the evils alluded to have arisen from this cause, they can only be remedied by emigration. Where, as generally happens, improvements are gradually and slowly introduced, the increased demand keeps pace with the increased production, so that no one is thrown out of employment, while all enjoy, in their own consumption, the benefit of the increased cheapness of the article.

As to our own country, Massachusetts, the State in which the population is most dense and the soil least productive, is also the wealthiest in the Union. This combination of circumstances settles the question as to the effect of the progress of population upon the reward of labor, unless some particular reasons can be found in the condition of that State for considering it as an exception to the rule rather than an illustration of it. In a community where taxation is very light, and trade comparatively free,—with the grain-growing countries of the west entirely so,—it is difficult to imagine any cause that should prevent the individual laborer from receiving his just proportion of the whole produce, or, in other words, should prevent the real rate of wages from being higher than

it is in the less populous parts of the Union. A slight observation of the condition of the State of Massachusetts, with reference to accumulated capital, public buildings, rail-roads, and other public improvements,—education and religious instruction,—learning and the arts,—navigation, commerce, and manufactures,—and the individual accommodation of the people in the way of lodging, clothing, food, and amusements, is sufficient to show that there is all the difference that might be expected, on any view of the subject, in her favor.

The difference on the other side in your estimate,—supposing it to be accurate,—must be accounted for, as I remarked before, by the fact that the western States are a grain-growing country. Good claret wine,—such as is commonly sold in our cities at half a dollar a bottle,—can be made in the south of France at about a cent a bottle. Supposing the wages of a French peasant to be about a *franc,* or twenty cents, a day, and those of a New England laborer about a dollar, the comparative reward of labor in the two countries, estimated in French wine, would be twenty bottles per day in France, and two in New England. Estimated in ice or granite, which have been pleasantly described as the only two natural products of Massachusetts, the reward of labor in that State, as compared with what it is in the west, would appear greater than it really is. But, without going into farther details on this subject, it is certain that, in a community which is really wealthier than another,—or, in other words, which receives regularly in return for its labor a larger amount of produce,— a comparatively lower rate of wages, if real, cannot be accounted for, as it must be on your system, by the supposition of a deficiency in the supply of the means of subsistence.

Before closing this letter, I will advert very briefly to one or two passages in yours, not material to the main argument, but involving some not unimportant errors in fact and opinion.

You say, incidentally, that a population of 640 to the square mile is physically impossible, " because the acre which, in this case, would be allotted to each individual, would be insufficient to supply him with food, clothing, fuel, and the other necessaries and comforts of life.'' This statement falls of itself, with the general proposition implied in it, that necessary supplies can only be obtained from the territory occupied by the party which is to use them. But, independently of this objection, the statement is liable to the still more direct and peremptory one, that the degree of density in population, which you suppose to be physically impossible, has been actually realized in various parts of the world. The present average population of the kingdom of Belgium is given in a statistical essay now before me, published at Brussels, in 1838, by the chief clerk in the department of finance, and which may be regarded as semi-official, at 125 to the 100 hectares of land, which is about one to every two acres, or 320 to the square mile. Some of the provinces of that kingdom have considerably more than the average density. East Flanders is represented, on the same authority, as having a population of 250 to the 100 hectares, or about double the average density. It reaches, of course, about 640 to the square mile,— the density which you suppose to be physically impossible. The population of Holland is, according to my recollection, still more dense than even this; but I have no document at hand from which I can draw the exact figures. That province is said to be the most populous region of equal extent in Christendom : and it must, as I should think, appear very singular to those who believe that the inhabitants of every part of the world can only subsist upon the direct produce of the territories they respectively occupy, that the most populous region should produce nothing, with the exception of cheese and butter, and the common garden vegetables, which is employed by the inhabitants as their usual means of subsistence.

You say, toward the close of your letter, that you '' do not think that any argument can be drawn from the supplies which great cities like London receive from the country. As a half or even a third of the population are sufficient to raise raw produce for the rest, and as the other operations of industry are better carried on in towns, the people of every country naturally distribute themselves into two portions, one in the country and the other in towns ; but whether in many small ones or a few large ones, must depend upon the rivers, harbors, and other localities, and on their commerce and manufactures. The progress of population tends to enlarge these cities, but, as we have seen, to lessen the supplies that can be exported, and consequently that can be imported.''

The argument drawn from the supplies furnished to large cities by the country is that, in every such case, a population occupying a more or less extensive territory, subsists wholly on supplies imported from abroad. In London, for example, a population of more than two millions occupies a territory of perhaps fifteen or twenty square miles in extent, which does not produce anything whatever that can be used as food. Every instance of this kind seems to me to be fatal to a theory which supposes that the inhabitants of every part of the globe must necessarily subsist upon the products of the soil they occupy, and rests upon that supposition as its sole foundation. I do not see that this argument, which appears to me entirely irresistible, is affected by your remarks, as quoted above. When you say '' that the progress of population, while it enlarges the cities, tends to lessen the supplies that can be exported, and consequently that can be imported,'' I understand you to mean that it tends to lessen the amount of agricultural produce which is furnished by the country to the towns. If this be your meaning, the remark is no doubt true, because a greater quantity will now be wanted for consumption in the country ; but this fact has no tendency to show that the population of cities is not supported entirely by supplies from without, or that whole provinces might not, if necessary, be supported in the same way. I agree with you in the opinion that the progress of population has, in general, a tendency to diminish the quantity of agricultural produce that can be exported ; but the articles which are exported, in exchange for provisions, by a country subsisting on supplies from abroad, are, in general, not the produce of agricultural but of manufacturing labor ; and the progress of population tends, as you remark in your letter, to augment very much the amount and the quality of this description of products. In exchange for these, any corresponding amount of imports of any kind that may be wanted can, of course, be procured.

I fear, my dear sir, that I have tasked your patience somewhat too severely. I trust, however, that you will consider the length of this letter as a proof of the respect that I feel for your opinions, and of my wish to show you that I have not come to a different conclusion without a full consideration of the subject. I should, of course, adopt, without hesitation, any correction of these conclusions that might appear to be necessary. If you notice any errors in the suggestions that I have now made, you would particularly oblige me by pointing them out. On the other hand, it would give me great pleasure to find that these suggestions have met your approbation, and have led you to take a view of the subject, which, I think, must be admitted by all to be more agreeable and satisfactory than the one stated in your letter.

I am, with great respect, my dear sir, very truly, your friend and obd't servant.

Signed,   A. H. EVERETT.

Hon. George Tucker

THE

UNITED STATES MAGAZINE,

AND

DEMOCRATIC REVIEW.

VOL. XVII.   NOVEMBER, 1845.   No. LXXXIX.

THE MALTHUSIAN THEORY.

DISCUSSED IN A CORRESPONDENCE BETWEEN ALEX. H. EVERETT AND PROF.
GEO. TUCKER, OF THE UNIVERSITY OF VIRGINIA.

(CONTINUED FROM OUR LAST.)

NO. V.

Professor Tucker to Mr. Everett.

University of Virginia, Feb. 22d, 1845.

MY DEAR SIR.—Your letter of the 29th of last month, in reply to mine written some eight or nine months since, has received my most attentive consideration ; and although you have dispelled whatever of hope I had indulged of vindicating in your eyes the soundness of my views on the subject of wages, I cannot but think that our opinions are not so wide apart as they at first seemed to be. It is true that we are distinctly opposed as to the effect produced by the progress of population upon the wages of labor, but since each admits several qualifications and exceptions to his general principle, the difference between us mainly amounts to this—what one regards as a general rule, the other regards as exceptions.

Still we differ on many incidental points both of fact and argument, as well as on their relative importance ; and I avail myself of your liberal and polite invitation to animadvert on these in defence of what appears to me to be the true theory of wages. In doing so I am not conscious of being actuated by another motive than a desire to ascertain the truth upon a subject at once intricate and important, though it is very possible that I am not exempt from that very common bias of wishing others to see with our eyes.

When, in my address to the National Institute, last Spring, I assumed the future decline of the wages of labor in the United States with their increasing density of population, according to a known law in political economy, I referred to the period when the whole of the best land should have been taken into cultivation, and consequently did not consider the principle as yet applicable to countries like this or New Holland, which possess a power of production far exceeding the wants of their present numbers. This exception was made in my letter to you, as I think (for retaining no copy of it, I am not certain) ; but I know that it was expressly made in the address, in which I stated, that while in other countries population was determined by the means of subsistence, here those means were determined by population. The liberal wages, therefore, which labor continues to obtain in the United States, do not at all conflict with the theory in question. Yet even here we already find some difference between the wages given in those portions of the country in which population is most dense, and where it is least so. According to a scale framed on evidence derived from members of the U. S. Senate, the the daily wages of ordinary labor in 1836 were less in New England than in the Western country, not only when estimated in bread and meat, *but also in money.* In New England the average price was 71¾ cents ; in Massachusetts 67 cents ; and in the Western free States 83⅓ cents.

In maintaining that wages decline with the increasing density of population, it seems to me that I merely asserted a corollary from the limited extent of the earth's productiveness and the physical and moral laws of man's nature. He is impelled by one of the strongest impulses to multiply his species, and as his numbers increase, so must also his means of subsistence. Now, after the best lands of a country are taken into cultivation, an addition of food to meet the wants of a farther accession of numbers, can be met only in the following ways :

1. By improvement in husbandry, whereby the same expenditure of labor and capital is made to yield a greater return.

2. By a resort to inferior soils.

3. By a further expenditure of capital producing a smaller proportionate return.

4. By importing raw produce from other countries.

I know of no mode in which the amount of human aliment in a country can be increased which will not fall under one of the foregoing heads. Now, of these, it is only the first that increases the quantity without increasing the price. Indeed, if the farther supply they produce exceed the demand from the supposed accession of numbers, then the price of raw produce will be reduced, and consequently the laborer receive a larger amount. Such excess of raw produce, however, is, according to experience, but short-lived, since mouths soon come into existence sufficient to consume it.

If the multiplying propensity still continue to act as we find that it has

everywhere done, after the best lands are taken into cultivation, and after the additional supply from improved husbandry is exhausted, the other three expedients must, in whole or in part, be resorted to, and every one of them supplies a diminished return to the same expense of labor, or, in other words, a fall of wages. And each of the three has been referred to by three different political economists of distinction to explain the gradual rise of rents from the gradual rise of raw produce— Ricardo making use of the resort to inferior soils in succession ; Mill to excessive expenditures of additional capital, and Senior to the necessity of drawing food from a greater distance. If these views are correct, it would follow that every increase of population, which derived its subsistence from either of the three last expedients, must be attended with a rise in the price of raw produce, and correspondent fall in the wages of labor.

But to this inference you make two objections. One is, that in estimating the laborer's wages we ought not to regard raw produce exclusively ; the other, that the rise in the price of raw produce, consequent on an increase of popoulation, is more than balanced by a fall in the price of manufactures ; and that by exchanging these for food in countries in which raw produce has not so risen, and manufactures not so fallen, a densely peopled country may obtain the supplies it requires at a less and less expense of labor.

As to the first objection, I would remark that there is probably no country in the world in which the value of the whole raw produce annually consumed does not exceed that of the manufactures. Such is certainly the fact in Great Britain and this country, as is shewn by authentic documents. But as the wealthy class consume a larger portion of manufactures, the laboring class consume less. It further appears, from an estimate made by Sir Frederic M. Edein, in 1796, that of the annual expenses of the family of a laborer (formed from a comparison of the expences of sixty-five families), the cost of provisions was £27 1s. 8d., out of an annual earning of £36 14s. 4d., or 73 per ct. And in 1823, according to Lowe's estimate, it was £27 1s. 8d. out of £39 2s. 7d., or 69 per ct. Now, when it is recollected that several irticles of consumption besides provisions, as leather, candles, &c., being the produce of the soil, must rise in piice with food, we may ascribe three-fourths, or 75 per cent., to be a moderate estimate of the proportion of raw produce consumed by the laborer in England ; and in those countries (comprehending all the rest of Europe, and all Asia and Africa) in which the condition of the laboring class is yet lower, the proportion is yet greater.

Nor is this all. The raw produce consumed by the laborer exceeds the manufactures yet more in importance than in amount. No improvement in the quality, or cheapness of the last can compensate him for a moderate privation in the article of food, or an increased difficulty in obtaining it. What solace would he find for coarser or scantier fare in having a shirt or two more, or of better quality, more or prettier cups and saucers, and better knives and forks ? Little or none, I conceive ; and it was both from its relative quantity and its importance to human happiness, that I made raw produce the measure of his real wages.

Your second objection rests upon an hypothesis, which I admit to be ingenious, and to afford your law of wages its most plausible support, yet it will not stand the test of close scrutiny. It seems to me to be equally repugnant to the principles of sound theory and to well-authenticated facts.

In the first place, your hypothesis *greatly overrates the effect of the supposed exchange* in reducing the cost of raw produce. It is manifest that in an isolated community no improvement in machinery or manufacturing skill can check the rise of such produce occasioned by increase of numbers. If two yards of cloth, or two pairs of stockings can be produced at the same expense of labor as was formerly required to produce one yard or one pair, the two will exchange for no more in the market than the one had done. And so for any further difference. It is immaterial what saving of labor or capital is effected. As soon as the improvement has lost its temporary character of monopoly, and becomes diffused, the article produced falls in price according to the amount of that saving, and it will take a proportionately greater amount of it to pur-

chase the same quantity of raw produce.

Let us, however, suppose that the same community has an unrestricted intercourse with other countries ; what, then, will be the effect on the price of raw produce ?

In those countries with which the manufacturing nation has always had commerce, her manufactures will continue to fall, as they have fallen at home, they yielding always the same average profit. But by reason of the greater cheapness of her manufactures, she may be able to open a traffic with other nations, which had not been previously profitable, and both sell her manufactures higher, and buy raw produce cheaper than she could at home. But in the same way that the profits of her labor-saving machines are soon equalized among manufactures, the extra profits of commerce are soon equalized among merchants ; and in no long time these channels of trade yield only the average profits of capital. So that the effect of these cheap manufactures is extended to other countries, and while they enable the nation possessing them to provide a farther supply of raw produce for its increasing numbers, they tend rather to check or retard the rise of that produce than to make it cheaper.

In accordance with these views, we find that in every part of the world the products of the Manchester looms have fallen in the same proportion as they have fallen in England, and that the price of grain in that country, notwithstanding its increased means of produce in more distant countries, and its improved means of transportation, has risen probably 100 per cent in a century. It rose from £1 15s. 4¾d. in 1725 (the average of ten years) to £3 18s. 8¼d. in 1825 (also the average of ten years) ; and although the average for the last ten years is probably less than it was in 1825, I have no doubt it is double the average price a century since.

A farther objection to your hypothesis is that the supply of food, which can be obtained by importation, is *inadequate* to the wants of an increasing population.

Of course I speak here not of small communities, but of such countries as England, France and the other European monarchies. The supplies thus to be drawn from abroad imply that the countries furnishing them have the means of subsistence beyond the wants of their own population, which is rarely the case, excepting when it has more than an average crop.

In the natural progress of society population and food seem everywhere to have gone on increasing *pari passu,* so that the numbers of every community have generally been up to their means of subsistence. And this has been quite as true in the earlier stages of society as in the more advanced.— The United States (with some other parts of the continent), and New Holland are exceptions to this general rule, because in them alone the means of producing food is in advance of the population. But in Europe, in Asia, and in Africa, comprehending probably nineteen-twentieths of the human race, the annual consumption of every community is very rarely short of its annual production; and the means of subsistence of a large majority of its members, whether they be nomadic or agricultural, or whether their agriculture is rude or highly improved, is obtained only by great efforts and unremitting labor. Nor is there any part of Europe in which there is regularly an annual surplus of grain, excepting Poland and Russia. But we can see a cause why the population of these countries has not kept pace with their means of subsistence. Their laboring classes are still serfs, who are made to raise wheat for their masters to exchange for foreign luxuries. Were they emancipated, it seems reasonable to suppose that towns and manufactures would grow up there as they have done in other parts of Europe, by means of which a demand would be afforded at home for all the food they could raise.

In the mean time, the quantity of grain afforded by them contributes little to support the growing population of Great Britain, their best customer. The average annual export of both wheat and rye from Poland to all parts of the world has been in 150 years but 279,000 quarters; and Jacob, sent by the British Government to ascertain the capacity of that country to furnish foreign supplies, states, that if the British ports were opened to Polish grain, the annual amount it would export would not exceed 350,000 to 450,000 quarters. Supposing this all to go to Great Britain, it would, at the usual allowance of one quarter to each per-

son, annually contribute less than one-fortieth of the bread consumed by its whole population, and less than one-eighteenth of (that consumed by) the addition it has received to its population in 40 years (7,593,140). The quantity of grain imported from Russia (principally, I presume, from Odessa), is that imported from Poland through Dantzic. The average annual import from the latter for 25 years (from 1801 to 1825) was 228,584 quarters, while that from Russia was only 117,902 quarters (McCulloch's Dict. Act. Corn Laws.)

The reason of this difference is to be found, not in the greater quantity exported from Dantzic, for there is commonly more than twice as much grain imported from Odessa, but the latter must be sent in the winter months, or it is liable to heat in the long voyage to Great Britain.

England receives grain from many other parts of Europe almost every year, though most of those very countries import, on an average, more than they export. But the excess of her imports from all countries above her total exports averaged 604,285 quarters in the ten years to 1819. In the succeeding years it averaged 368,231 quarters; and in the six years succeeding, 615,738 quarters. The highest amount is equal, according to McCulloch, only to about four days' consumption of the United Kingdom for all purposes. (See Com. Dict., p. 417). The greatest amount which Great Britain ever received in one year was 3,541,809 quarters (in 1831), less than one-fourteenth of her annual consumption.

If, then, the richest and most commercial and maratime nation in the world has never been able, when under the pressure of unwonted scarcity, to obtain but a small proportion of her subsistence from abroad, how could she be able to procure an adequate supply if her population were doubled or trebbled? It could not be procured in Europe, unless we suppose that its governments would consent to starve a part of her people for her calicoes and cutlery.

It is true that under the relative circumstances between Great Britain and the United States, the one producing grain at a low expense of labor and capital, and the other affording the best market for it in the world, a trade in that article often takes place ; and, were the British Corn Laws repealed, it would be greatly extended. Yet no large addition would be made to the demand here without considerably raising the price ; and the peculiar circumstances of this country, which render raw produce cheap, are gradually passing away ; and, at the rate at which we are increasing, after allowing for a gradual diminution of that rate, in less than a century all the best land will be taken into cultivation. The price of raw produce will then necessarily rise, and gradually approximate to that in Europe.

It must farther be recollected that even the moderate supplies now obtained in European countries, are not likely to continue unabated. The same wants will, by quickening invention and skill, hasten the progress of manufactures, and the same tending to multiply will enlarge the domestic demand foor food ; so that the exchange of manufactured for agricultural products will be more and more circumscribed, and less profitable. It is from these changes in civil society, ever slowly but steadily going on, that have arisen many of the great revolutions in commerce, of which history informs us. And the progressive increase of art, of capital, and consequently of population, is hastened by nothing more than this very commerce.

We have evidence of this progress and the consequent rise in the price of raw produce in the returns made by the English Consuls, as reported by Porter's Tablet (Part 5, p. 448). According to those returns of the prices of wheat in some twenty places, scattered over the North, the South, the East, the West and the Middle of Continental Europe, it appears that in all of them that species of grain had risen in price in the course of a century, and in several instances within half that time. It further appears from reference to other parts of the same authentic work, that the importation of Great Britain from some of these places had not only not increased, but had actually ceased, except when an unusually short crop at home made her willing to pay an extra price abroad. Even at Dantzic, where the increase of population and wealth until lately has been less than in most parts of Europe, for the reason

already mentioned, the price of wheat has risen as follows :

From 1770 to 1779 the price was	33s.	9d.	the qua'r.
1780 " 1789 "	33	10	"
1790 " 1799 "	43	8	"
1800 " 1809 "	60	0	"
1810 " 1819 "	55	4	"

Thus showing a rise of 64 per cent in 40 years.

Another objection to your expedient of importing food for an increasing population is, that it overlooks the *practical difficulties* from *distance* and *cost of transport.*

Aware that the supply from any one country may be exhausted, you say that in that event Great Britain may resort to another, and so on in succession, until she had put in requisition the productive power of the whole globe. But her power of obtaining supplies lies within far narrower limits. It must be recollected that provisions are consumed in making provisions and in transporting them from place to place, and that, therefore, they cannot be transported to a greater distance than will absorb their value after paying for the labor and capital expended in making them. Now, where grain has to be subjected to ordinary land carriage, the limit is soon reached. In our rough woods in Virginia, the expense of wagonage is about one cent. a mile per bushel ; so that, at the present price, after allowing a very moderate return to the producer, it could not be wagoned thirty miles to market, and seventy-five or eighty miles would absorb its whole value, and leave nothing to reward the labor of producing it.

But by far the larger part of the productive lands of the world are unapproachable by water, and, of course, suppose the necessity of land carriage. Virginia is, for example, as well provided with navigable rivers as most countries, yet three-fourths, and perhaps nine-tenths of her soil is accessible only by land carriage. This circumstance makes wheat in a large part of the State an unprofitable article of culture. The effect of land carriage is, of course, variable. depending partly on the distance and partly on the price of wheat.

But by the new improvements of railroads, these impediments to transportation are continually growing less. That is true; but even by these the carriage is not gratuitous; and I apprehend that the value of a barrel of flour, after allowing the lowest return to its producers, would be commonly absorbed by the cost of transporting it by railroad two or three hundred miles. Even these railroads only lessen the necessity of wagonage—they do not dispense with it altogether; and much of the produce they convey has been previously subjected to a heavy charge of land carriage. It is the same with the produce conveyed to market by canals.

Even where the transportation is by water, and in the cheapest mode of shipping, distance considerably enhances the price. Thus, when wheat is only 39s. 4d. at Dantzic, it costs 66s. 4d. at London, according to the report of the Inspector General in 1841; 24s. 9d. at Odessa, and 49s. 11d. at Rotterdam. As it was all subjected to the same duty, the difference of price is to be referred solely to the difference of distance. This, then, is 10s. 7d. per quarter more from Dantzic than from Rotterdam, and 14s. 5d. from Odessa than from Dantzic. When we recollect that wheat is brought to Odessa in wagons, it is clear that the price of 24s. 9d. per quarter yields a very small pittance to the cultivator, and that it would require no great addition to the distance to leave him, at this price, nothing at all. Nor is there any part of the world from which Great Britain can now derive grain at the distance of 3,000 miles, except the United States, which supply, as we have seen, cannot be permanent.

The transportation alone would present an insuperable obstacle in the way of the large and constantly increasing supply that you consider practicable. Mr. G. R. Porter, who is an advocate for the repeal of the British Corn Laws, and, consequently, not inclined to underrate the benefit of importing foreign corn, affirms, that to supply the United Kingdom with wheat alone (the additional quantity wanted, if the population were merely doubled), would require more than twice the shipping that now enters their ports; and to bring to their shores every article of agricultural produce in the same abundance as at present, would probably give constant occupation to the *mercantile navy of the whole world.* He thinks that though an inconsiderable state or colony may be habitually dependent on

the soil of other countries for its food, this can never be the case with a numerous people; and that it is impossible that any great accessions to its numbers can be supported by importations from abroad. These considerations suggested the remark that every country (meaning of the ordinary extent) must draw the chief part of its food from its own soil; nor do I know on the globe a single exception.

It thus appears that no improvements in manufacturing industry can prevent the rise in the price of raw produce at home, nor long or materially affect its price abroad; that the supplies by importation must be insufficient for the wants of any large accessions to to the population; and that even these must be obtained at a continually advancing price; from which it would follow, that the general law of the gradual rise of raw produce and fall of wages, with the progress of society, can no more be controlled by importations of food than by any other human means, except that of arresting the farther increase of numbers.

By way of testing the correctness of these views, let us refer to the real wages received by the laborer in Great Britain at different stages of her increase, according to Porter's Progress of the Nation:

From 1742 to 1752 the wages of common labor were 102 pints of wheat per week.
" 1761 to 1770, 90 "   "   "   "
" 1788 to 1790, 80 "   "   "   "
" 1795 to 1799, 65 "   "   "   "
" 1800 to 1808, 60 "   "   "   "

Since 1808, they have undoubtedly risen, and in 1823 they had, according to Lowe, again reached to 80 pints. But they have since fallen below that, and seem to be still declining. If, then, in Great Britain, the country, which, of all others, most requires food from abroad, and which has the most ample means of paying for it, and transporting it, we find the real wages of labor declining while population is increasing, we may consider the fact as an *experimentum crucis* that importation can have no effect in *arresting* the decline of wages, whatever it may have in retarding it.

But even if adequate and increasing supplies of food by importation were practicable, there would be this fatal objection to the principle that the wages of labor increase with the density of population—*that it could be true in some countries only, because it was not true in others.*

It is obvious that to the same extent to which some countries *import* food, others *export* it. All cannot be importers. Now, if importations are necessary for wages to increase with our increasing population, it follows that in those countries which do not import, *if the population continued to increase* (as it may and probably will do where the laboring class has not yet reached the cheapest aliment), *wages must fall.* Supposing the people of the world to increase with its food, as they ever have done, if some receive more than an average share, others must receive less; as at a gaming table, the sum lost must equal the sum won.

Having thus given you my views on the subject of wages uninterruptedly and more fully than I had permitted myself to do before, I propose to take a special notice of particular passages in your letter in which we all chance to disagree.

You say that the facts on which I rely, that wages are higher in the United States than in England, and higher in England than in India, "are not easily reconciled with the supposition that an increase of population regularly occasions a comparative scarcity." I have puzzled myself not a little to discover on what ground you could have seen or supposed any incompatibility between the facts I cited and the principle I maintained, but have not been able to find any, unless it is in confounding two propositions—one that I did make with one that I did not—or at least confounding the rate of *present* increase with the *amount* of past increase.

The proposition that I assert and you deny is, that wages decline with increasing density. For the purpose of testing the principle by facts, we may compare the wages of labor in the same country at different periods, and see whether they have fallen as population has increased, or otherwise. This I have done, so far as I had materials; and in support of my views I relied upon the example of Great Britain. I next, by way of farther illustration, compared one country with another, to see whether here also wages are highest where population is least dense, and lowest where it is most dense; and find-

ing that to be the case on comparing the United States, England and India, I naturally regard the fact as confirming my principle. If, however, the opposite theory were true, wages ought to be higher in Bengal than in England, because population is there relatively more dense, and, for the same reason, ought to be higher in England than in the United States. Though wages are higher in England than they are in India, it does not follow that they are not falling in the former; and though wages are at the lowest point of depression in India, it does not follow that they have not been higher; yet unless these strange inferences could be drawn, there is no repugnance between my facts and my doctrine. In like manner, I referred to different parts of the United States, as affording farther, though not such striking evidence, of the same principle. Thus in New England, where population is most dense, real wages are lowest; and in the Western States, where population is least dense, wages are highest. The *rate* of increase, which is a very different thing from the amount of previous increase, being mainly dependent on real wages, ought, like them, to be universally as density of population; though to this rule there are many exceptions, according as the laboring class more or less subsists on animal food—on the dearer or cheaper kinds of grain, or on potatoes. On this subject it is relative and not absolute density that is referred to. One country that is barren or rudely cultivated, may be as densely peopled for its productiveness with 50 to the square mile as another with 200.

Notwithstanding this misconception of my reasoning of the doctrine as to the difference between the wages of labor in England and India—a country abounding in unreclaimed jungle, and most wretchedly cultivated, yet teeming with people—you distinctly admit that the difference between wages in this country and England is a contradiction to your theory, and you refer the discrepancy to political causes.

I am not disposed to underrate the influence of these on the prosperity of nations, and readily admit that an unrestrained trade in corn in England, a radical change in its system of poor laws, and a lighter taxation, would directly benefit the condition of its laboring class. Yet as to the wages of labor, I cannot see that such changes would have more than a temporary effect. The tendency of the amelioration would be, to give a new spring to population; and though its increase should not be accelerated, yet, at its recent rate of increase, the laborer's earnings would soon be reduced to their present amount. The only remedies for the evil are of a moral character—greater pride of personal independence, a higher standard of domestic comfort, and a consequent forbearance to marry until the means of supporting a family are obtained.

While the experience of England is opposed to your theory of wages—they having *fallen* there though population has *increased*—yet it may also appear not conformable to mine, considering that the fall in the rate of wages has been far less than the increase of population, and that the two have not been strictly concurrent. Yet it must be remembered that the quantity of arable land has there received an increase of 6,000,000 acres by inclosure acts passed within the last 50 or 60 years; that the husbandry of the country has experienced prodigious improvement, and now approaches its maximum of productiveness; that taxation, since the long wars with France, bears more (less?) heavily on the laborer than it did, and a part of it goes to swell the amount of wages he receives. The great increase of capital, and, consequently, the fall of profits and the improved means of transport, have also contributed to increase the population without proportionally reducing the wages of labor. Nor ought I to omit in this enumeration the increased facility of buying from abroad that has been bestowed by the great inventions of Watt, Hargrave and Arkwright. The meliorating effect of these improvements on the comfort of the poorest cottages is very great, and can never be diminished; but as to the mitigating influences on the price of food, they are passing away; and if her people continue to increase, so must increase their penury and wretchedness.

But you refer with confidence to Massachusetts, to show that an increase of population is accompanied by an increase of wages. In answer to this, I have already shown that they were not so high as in the Middle States, or the Western in 1836, when reckoned either in bread, meat, or money. They have probably since risen, and, I presume, are at this time as high as in most of the States. Yet it must not be forgotten that she is now enjoying advantages that she does not owe altogether to the density of her population. She has at this time all the benefits both of the restrictive system and that of free trade. She derives from the Constitution of the United States an unrestricted trade to every part of the Union, most portions of which are far inferior to her in ability to manufacture, but superior to her in cheapness of raw material. She can thus procure food from them cheaper than she can raise it, and have a large and growing market for her manufactures; and farther, by means of legal restrictions, foreign rivals, who might, by their cheaper labor and cheaper capital, undersell her, are either excluded from the same domestic market or subjected to burdens from which she is exempt. It is on these accounts that she is now experiencing unexampled prosperity. This I am far from envying. On the contrary, I look at these consequences of her enterprise, skill, industry, and political good fortune, with pleasure and pride, for my feelings are truly national. But were the tariff repealed or the confederacy dissolved, it cannot be doubted that many of her factories, which now yield to their proprietors a profit of 12 or 15 per cent. on their capital, must then stop, or put up with reduced profits. Thousands of her citizens, now earning liberal wages, would then emigrate to the fertile lands of the west.

Nor need we require political changes to bring about a fall in the wages of her labor. Domestic rivals in manufacturing industry will naturally rise up at home, and bring down her profits to the common level; and the raw produce which now finds its way from the fertile valley of the Ohio, will, in less than a century, be consumed there. That favored spot will become the Flanders of the United States, and its redundant population will furnish the rest of the United States with its laces and its cambrics, its cutlery—perhaps its porcelain and its silks. In estimating the rate of wages, you think we ought to take into account the condition of the "community at large," not only as to the necessaries of life, but also as to its " comforts and luxuries—lodging, clothing, fire, food, machinery of all kinds, professional aid, education, religious instruction, and amusements of all description." On this question we must not confound the laboring class with the wealthy class, nor the earnings of labor with the benefits of civilization. A part of the sources of enjoyment of which you speak, belong, in every community, exclusively to the richer portion. Of this character are the luxuries of life, a large proportion of its comforts, and its most refined amusements. From these the laboring class are almost as completely shut out in London or Paris as they would be on the frontier of Iowa or Missouri. It can add but little to their happiness to see another going to the opera, the concert, or the exhibition room, from which poverty and rags exclude them. And though even the common laborer may greet his eyes with a *sight* of the Tuileries or the Arc de Triomphe, yet, I imagine, there are thousands in Paris who would agree never to see these magnificent objects in consideration of a single substantial meal. And to consider the laborer's share of the benefits arising from art, science, and civilization—even were it larger than unfortunately it is (as wages?)—would be to confound terms, and to use diet of " wages" in a sense that we never allude to it. By the word, I understand that reward the laborer receives from the employer for the work done, and, consequently, it is not meant to comprehend those casual benefits that are gratuitous—are derived from the civilization and improvement of the community in which he lives, which he shares with the common beggar, and which are but as dust in the balance when weighed against the necessaries of life. I do not refer to the cheaper and better clothing, utensils, furniture, which the laborer can obtain in exchange for a part of his wages. This class of articles is, so far as it goes, a real addition to his wages, for it gives him more enjoyment in return for less labor. But I think, for the reason already stated, that what he gains does not compensate him for what he loses by reason of great density of population : in a word, that the amount of his compensation can be better measured by the amount of the article of common food he receives than by any-

thing else ; and whenever men can subsist on *wine*, or *tea*, or *ice*, or *granite*, then these articles will be as good a measure of wages as wheat, and not until then.

You seem to dissent from my proposition that men everywhere increase more or less rapidly according to the greater or less facility of procuring subsistence ; yet, in support of my opinion, we find that in the United States, where food is most easily procured, the increase is most rapid ; that in England, since they have added so largely to the arable land, and fertilized it by sending to the Pampas of South America for the bones of slaughtered animals, and whole fleets for guano, &c., her population has increased more in 50 years than it had done in two centuries before ; that in every part of Northern and Middle Europe, and a part of the South, population has, of late years, been steadily increasing with the improvements in husbandry ; that even in Bengal its population is visibly increasing with an improving husbandry. All these facts seem to assure us that population and food go hand in hand. It is a farther confirmation of the same fact, that in England and France the number of marriages regularly increased or declined with the rise or fall in the price of food; as is shown by Mr. Porter in his progress. (Vol. III., ch. 4.)

It is likely enough that I erred in roundly asserting that a population of 640 to a square mile was physically impossible. I still believe it of every country in the temperate zones ; but it is possible that *within the tropics*, where vegetation is uninterrupted, a country without mountains or deserts, inhabited by a people requiring little food or clothing, using no animal food, and being without horses, might attain this density, or yet greater. The island of Barbadoes has already reached it, or very nearly approached to it, though I believe it receives large supplies of grain and flour from this country. But I am not able to see wherein this error was important in our inquiries. A country having but 10 persons to the square mile, would, after six duplications, have a population of 640 to the square mile. This I considered a greater density than it was possible to attain; and I assumed this because Mr. Gray, that opponent to Mr. Malthus, whom he most respected, considered that two acres to each person (320 to the square mile) was the limit of extreme density in Great Britain. But if I underrated the capacities of the soil to sustain man, I had only to assume seven duplications instead of six, and have taken 1.280 to the square mile; the argument was the same in either case. In point of fact, however, with the exception already made, I am still inclined to think that I have assumed a limit which will never be reached. It is true that particular portions of a country may have an inhabitant for every acre, or near it; but it is only the whole civil community to which my remark applies. And although East Flanders has near that population (for it has not yet quite reached it), though Lancaster county, in England, still larger than East Flanders, has a population of more than 900 to the square mile, yet it would be no more proper to consider these as disproving my proposition than the city of London, since they, as certainly as that metropolis, could not support their present population unless they were merely parts of larger communities; nor is there a country in the world of sufficient extent for an independent state, which has a population much beyond half that which I had considered as its utmost limit. The population of Belgium, according to an official statement, in 1838, was 352 to the square English mile; that of Holland, 225; of England, leaving out Wales and Scotland, 297, in 1841.

As to the passage which you quote from my letter relative to great cities, my meaning has been misapprehended by you, because it was carelessly expressed. *Laboro esse brevis, fio obscurus.* I meant to say, that most countries can furnish subsistence for twice or thrice as many persons as are necessary to cultivate them, and that it is an importance to the question between us whether the residue remains in the country or congregate in towns, and in many small towns or a few large ones; that the extraordinary density in these last is compensated by the inferior density in the country, where it subsisted on its domestic supplies; and that as to importations, the same progress of population, which enlarges the growth of these cities, also tends to lessen the supplies that can be import-

ed *from other countries,* and, consequently, those that can be imported into the cities in question; as I had previously argued. Thus, to make the application, so far as London derived its food from English soil, its excess, beyond the average density, would be balanced by a corresponding deficiency in the country; and that the less Poland, and other parts of Europe, were able to export, the less London could import; and as, according to the wonted progress of population, those countries might be presumed to be less and less able to export, and, eventually, not to export at all, so must be the power of London to import.

Your doctrine that all the materials of human happiness increase with population, is, I admit, very gratifying to the philanthropist; but, like the visions of an elixir of life, of perpetual motion, of universal peace, &c., they must yield to the stubborn facts which prove them false. Looking on man with the eyes of sober truth, we find him endowed with appetites and passions that are at once the source of his purest enjoyments and occasionally the cause of suffering and evil. Urged to multiply his numbers, compelled to earn his food by the sweat of his brow, or by tasking his mind, he finds the evils of life increased and its goods diminished, if he admits too many partners to share with him in the fruits of the soil. Yet I mean not to say that this tendency is *necessarily* productive of evil; and I differ from Malthus in the force of the proper correction—prudential restraint—which I incline to think, in an enlightened and well regulated community, will always keep down population to the point that admits of substantial comfort. So that while you think that the happiness of mankind will be indefinitely increased by his indulging in the multiplying propensity, I think it is best promoted by the moral part of his nature, and by subjecting that propensity to the control of his reason and foresight.

In conclusion, I will remark that though in this discussion neither should convince the other, as is very probable, seeing that the main question involves many others, which may be seen under different and even opposite aspects, yet it cannot but be gratifying to us to find that, in carrying on the controversy, neither of us has lost his temper.

Should you be disposed to prolong it, I should like to see my first letter, that I may ascertain how far I have failed to give to some of my remarks the requisite qualifications, or to have expressed them with precision. But not wishing to impose on you the trouble of having it copied, I will ask the favor of you to send me the original.

I am, with great respect, dear sir, your friend and obedient servant,

(Signed,)   GEORGE TUCKER.

Hon. A. H. Everett.

NO. VI.

Mr. Everett to Professor Tucker.

Washington, D. C., March 17, 1845.

DEAR SIR,—I have read with attention your letter of the 22d ult., and am greatly obliged to you for noticing with so much care my request for information in regard to the grounds of your opinions upon the question we are discussing. I have no doubt that by comparing our ideas upon it, though neither of us may, perhaps, convince the other, we may both obtain a clearer and more precise view of the subject.

In replying to my last letter, you do not, if I understand you rightly, contest the truth of the principle which I undertake to establish—viz., that the decline in the value of the produce of manufacturing labor, resulting from the progress of population, naturally brings with it a corresponding decline in the value of agricultural produce, excepting so far as the latter is counteracted by the increase in the cost of transportation. You rest your objections to my conclusion mainly on the ground that the cost of transporting agricultural produce is too great to admit of its being carried in large quantities to any great distance. In regard to this point, you say that the cost of transportation to any considerable distance would " absorb the value of the article," and that the trade would, of course, become impracticable.

This remark seems to imply that the value of the article at the place where it is wanted, is determined by some cause, other than the cost of production and transportation, and that if the latter equal or exceed the value so determined, the trade ceases. On the commonly received, and, as I had supposed, undisputed theory of prices, the value of the article at the place where

it is wanted is determined by the cost of production and transportation. This being an increase in the cost of transportation only increases to the price to the consumer, and leaves to the producer and carrier the same profit as before. So far as wages are regulated by the value of agricultural products, a positive increase in their price as paid by the consumer would, of course, be attended by a fall of wages. But, in this case, the effect of the increased cost of transportation in changing prices, is counterbalanced by the diminished value of the manufactured articles given in exchange ; so that the general result is a positive decline, instead of positive increase in the price of agricultural produce paid by the consumer, and consequently an actual rise instead of fall in the rate of wages. On the estimate made in my letter, where the cost of transportation both ways is taken at 50 per cent on the capital invested, the fall in the price of agricultural produce, and the consequent rise in the rate of real wages, would be also 50 per cent.

I have before me a statement taken from returns, made by order of the British Parliament, in 1841, of the quantity of grain which could be obtained from fifteen of the principal ports of the Continent of Europe, if English markets were thrown open—the price of wheat at each, and the freight thence to London. In this statement the average price of wheat at the fifteen ports is given at 40s., and the average freight to London at 4s. 9¾d., or about ten per cent on the value. The freight and charges on the outward voyage are of course, much less in proportion to the value of the cargo, which would consist generally of articles much less bulky than wheat. But assuming that they also amount to 10 per cent, the total cost of transportation both ways would be equal to 20 per cent on the capital invested. In my letter to you I estimated it at 50 per cent, which, it seems, is a good deal too high. I also estimated the decline on the value of manufactures, resulting from the doubling of the population, in a country where the land is already pretty well taken up, at 100 per cnt. On this supposition, and taking the cost of transportation both ways at 20 per cent instead of 50 per cent, the actual decline in the value of agricultural produce would be 30 per cent, and real wages, so far us they are regulated by the value of agricultural produce, would rise in the same proportion.

But this estimate is as much too low as the other was too high, at least if we can draw any conclusion from the case of Great Britain. During the last half century, while the population has been doubling itself in that country, the improvements in methods and machinery are seriously estimated at equivalent to the labor of 300,000,000 or 800,000,000 of men. The consequent increase in the productiveness of labor, and decline in the value of its products are, of course, equal, on the lowest of these estimates, to 3000 per cent, and on the highest to 8000 per cent. I take them at only one hundred per cent, which is certainly moderate enough, but still, as I have shewn, brings out an actual rise in real wages of 80 per cent. Without insisting on the minutes accuracy of these estimates, it is quite apparent that the decline in the value of the manufactured articles given in exchange for the agricultural produce imported, must be far more than sufficient to cover the cost of transporting the latter from a distance, and that the general result of the progress of population must be a rise and not a fall of real wages.

You object, in addition, that independently of the cost of transportation, the quantity of provisions, that could be obtained from a distance, would not correspond with the wants of a populous community. But on the usually received principles of political economy, the supply of every article naturally keeps pace with the effectual demand; and there would, of course, be no deficiency in the quantity of provisions, wherever there were other articles of equal value to be given in exchange for them, until the whole productive power of the globe should have been exhausted—a contingency, which, for the present purpose, may be left entirely out of the question.

In order to simplify the discussion, and bring it more directly to a point, I confine myself in this letter, as I did in the preceding one to the main argument, omitting all considerations of a subsidiary character. I will advert for a moment in conclusion, to your comments upon my remark, that in estimating the amount of the reward of labor, we ought to take into view the state of the community in

reference to the comforts and luxuries of life, as well as the sum actually paid to the laborer under the name of wages. You say that you "understand by wages the reward which the laborer receives from his employer for the work done, and that you do not comprehend in it, the casual benefits that are gratuitous, and are derived from the civilization and improvement of the society in which he lives."

On this point there would be, I apprehend, on comparison of ideas, no material difference of opinion between us. In speaking of the reward of labor, or wages, we both, of course, mean real and not merely nominal wages, and by real wages we both understand the amount of the necessaries and comforts of life, which the laborer is able to command with the money paid to him by his employer. Now, although the money price of labor is not affected by an increase in its productiveness, or by any circumstances except such as affect the state of the currency, yet if by the effect of an increase in the productiveness of laber resulting from the progress of population, and the consequent increased cheapness of the necessaries and comforts of life, the laborer is able to purchase with the same nominal wages twice or thrice as large a quantity of these as he would before, it is apparent that his real wages are augmented in the same proportion. You admit this so far as clothing, furniture, and other manufactured articles enter into his consumption ; but you suppose that the advantage which he gains in this respect is more than counterbalanced by the increased difficulty resulting from the same cause, in procuring provisions. I have endeavored to show that in this article, as well as in all others, there is not only no increase, but an actual decline in value, in consequence of the progress of population. Supposing this to be proved, it follows that the real wages of the laborer are increased in direct proportion to the progress of population ; and he may either employ the additional amount of the necessaries and comforts of life which he can now command in improving his mode of living, or he may live as as he did before, and economise the balance of his revenue. Even the accumulations that appear to be gratuitous, and are shared by the common beggar, such as roads and free schools, must be reckoned as a part of the laborer's real wages, because they are maintained out of the public treasury, which is supplied by a deduction from the wages of labor.

The money wages of the laborer in New England are somewhat lower, on your estimate, than those of a laborer in the Western States, and the difference, estimated in wheat, is greater than in money. But the money wages received by the laborer in New England represent for him a comfortable and well-furnished house—good food and clothing—a variety of manufactured articles of use, comfort and luxury—good roads—schools for his children—religious institutions, books and public amusements. At the West, a somewhat larger amount of nominal wages represents a log cabin, with scarcely any furniture—plenty of Indian meal, meat and whiskey—a small supply of manufactured articles at high prices—no roads—no schools—few books—few churches, and no public amusements. The difference between these two modes of living, in favor of the laborer of New England, constitutes the increase in less real wages, resulting from the greater density of population ; and if he choose to content himself with the comforts that are enjoyed at the West, he may realize this difference in money ; and even there will enjoy many important advantages, such as free schools for his children, which he could not enjoy under other circumstances, and which constitute a part of his real wages.

It is true that the most expensive accommodations of all kinds, afforded by a highly civilized state of society, are enjoyed exclusively by the rich. This is only saying that the individuals, whose labor is most productive, or who, in other words, receive the highest real wages, are able to command the greatest amount of the necessaries and comforts of life. This is, of course, a mere trueism, or rather an identical proposition. But this fact has no tendency to show that the real wages of all classes of laborers are not higher in a highly improved and populous community, than in one of a different character. Indeed the power of the rich to surround themselves with comforts and luxuries is much less dependent upon the state of the society in which they live, than

that of the less favored members of the community. A Russian or Polish nobleman lives upon his estates as luxuriously as a British peer, at his residence in London. But it is only in the midst of a dense population that the common citizen is able to afford himself accommodations of a similar, though generally less expensive kind, but which, in some cases, from the mere fact of their being shared by the multitude, are actually superior to the most expensive of an exclusive character that wealth can procure. Thus, the Queen of England finds it convenient to make use of the common railroad in preference to travelling with post horses in her own carriage ; so that the common citizen in England derives from the density of the population advantages for travelling, which the Queen is glad to share with him, from sheer inability to procure such as are equally good for her exclusive use by any application of the immense amount of means which she has at her disposal. And so of other cases of a similar kind.

I presume that you would agree with me in most of these remarks, and that there would be no great difference of opinion between us in regard to the effect of the increased productiveness of labor in raising the rate of real wages, although the money price may remain the same—excepting so far as this effect is counterbalanced by the increased cost and difficulty of procuring provisions. The extent to which this cause would probably operate seems to be the only important question upon which we are at issue. It is obviously one of fact rather than of principle ; and I venture to hope that you will think the remarks that I have made upon it in the earlier part of this letter, not wholly undeserving of your attention.

Agreeably to your desire, I return you the first of your two letters. You would oblige me by sending me the original, or a copy, of my first short letter to you. I shall be at this place most of the time until I sail for China, and will thank you to address to me, under cover, to the Department of State.

I am, dear sir, very truly and respectfully your friend and obedient servant,

Signed,   **A. H. EVERETT.**
Hon. George Tucker.

(To be continued in our next number.)

THE

UNITED STATES MAGAZINE,

AND

DEMOCRATIC REVIEW.

Vol. XVII.   DECEMBER, 1845.   No. XC.

THE MALTHUSIAN THEORY,

DISCUSSED IN A CORRESPONDENCE BETWEEN ALEX. H. EVERETT AND PROF. GEO. TUCKER, OF THE UNIVERSITY OF VIRGINIA.

(CONCLUDED FROM OUR LAST.)

NO. VII.

Professor Tucker to Mr. Everett.

University of Virginia, April 28, 1845.

DEAR SIR,—Your letter of the 17th of last month, which, however, did not reach me till more than four weeks after its date, would have received an immediate reply but for the recent disturbances among our students. I have ever since been wholly engaged in assisting to detect, or investigate, or punish these offences. I return you my first letter, and, agreeably to your request, send you copies of yours, in the hope that they may come to hand before you embark for China.

I will now trouble you with some explanations of those points of my letter of the 22d of February, which you seem to have greatly misapprehended; and I cannot but fear that, in the more pressing concerns of business, you have scarcely yet found time to give my voluminous epistle and its dry details a thorough perusal. I never meant to admit that " the decline in the value of the products of manufacturing labor, resulting from the progress of population, naturally brings with it a corresponding decline in the value of agricultural produce, except so far as the latter is counteracted by the increase in the cost of transportation." On the contrary, I stated, and endeavored to show, by facts as well as argument, that the progressive cheapness of manufactures can have but a small, a par-

tial, and a temporary effect in *retarding* the increasing difficulty of procuring food for an augmenting population; and, consequently, that " the gradual rise of raw produce and fall of wages with the progress of society, can no more be controlled by importations of food than by any other human means, excepting that of arresting the further increase of numbers."

Nor was my objection to your expedient of importing food confined to its cost. I urged three or four objections, any one of which I regarded as fatal; and lastly, I maintained that in admitting the necessity of importing provisions from abroad to meet the demands of an increasing population, you virtually surrender the question between us as to the general law of wages.

The simplest and fairest mode of determining whether the increasing density of numbers tends to raise or to lower wages, is, as it seems to me, to consider the course of an isolated country, depending wholly on its own resources, and in such a country you agree provisions must rise, and, of course, the largest part of the laborer's real wages must fall. If, however, we go to the other extreme, and consider the whole world as one community, you will also agree that the expedient of importation cannot be resorted to. It is then only those civil communities which have commerce with others, that can profit by the expedient. But since for every country that imports there must be another that exports, and some may be presumed neither to import nor export, it follows that the importing countries cannot be the greater number. As then the condition which you admit to be necessary to a continued rise of wages with an increase of population, is impracticable by a country limited to its own resources for food, by the whole world, regarded as one community, and by the greater number of the separate civil communities, your rule, on your own grounds, is not the general rule ; but the cases in which it may be true must be regarded as exceptions. Accordingly, the number of countries which habitually import part of the food consumed by the laboring class, is comparatively small, the supplies thus obtained are not likely to continue ; and they cannot permanently increase. But further,—with all the aid afforded by this temporary source, I know of no country in the world, except the few under the peculiar circumstances of the United States, in which wages, that is, real wages, estimated in meat and bread, have not risen (quere, *fallen*) with the increased density of population.

In answer to my remark that the cost of transporting provisions from any considerable distance " would absorb the value of the article," you rely on the received theory of prices, that the value of the article at the place where it is wanted is determined by the cost of production and transportation. But my proposition, so far from being in conflict with that theory, is a corollary from it.

There is a peculiarity in the production and transport of provisions, at which I thought it sufficient to hint, which makes the theory in question apply to them in a different way from that in which it applies to other commodities. A cask of wine, a chest of tea, or a bale of cloth, may be transported by water and land to the antipodes of those who produced it, and bring a price sufficient to repay the accumulated cost of production and conveyance, if it could not be obtained on easier terms. But there is a limit to the transport of provisions, which they cannot pass, let the price at the place where they are wanted be what it may. Human food must be consumed in the production and transport of that very food ; and after repaying the cost of production, and the ordinary profits of trade, it obviously cannot be transport-

ed to a greater distance than would be sufficient to consume the residue. It involves a contradiction, a moral impossibility, to suppose wheat habitually transported to another country, when a greater quantity of wheat or its equivalent would be consumed in the production or transportation. Whenever, then, the distance is great enough to produce this result, importation ceases. Thus Indian corn could not be wagoned to a market at a distance requiring ten days to travel it, or 180 miles, however high the price at that market, if in that time the horses would consume, as they probably would, one-half the load, and, of course, the other half in returning, even were the owner content to lose the value at the place of departure, his own time, &c. Or we may take an illustration from ice, one of the products of Massachusetts. It is gradually melting away, and, whatever may be its price abroad, the trade that may be carried on in this article must be short of the distance when it would be all dissolved. And although your very ingenious and enterprizing countrymen have succeeded in conveying it to Calcutta, yet they would find no tanner's bark, which would check the consumption of food, which is inseparable from the production and transport of food.

This is one reason among several others why every country of tolerable extent is compelled to rely upon its own inherent resources for the principal supply of its food.

A word or two on those improvements in skill and machinery in Great Britain, on which you so much rely in maintaining that the wages of labor *rise* with the increase of population. Without stopping to show, as I might easily do, that the notion of the gain or saving effected by these improvements, being equivalent to the labor of 800 millions of men, or even of 300 millions, is wild and hyperbolical in the extreme ; and without insisting on the fact that more sober estimates have reduced the number to 20 or 25 millions, I will merely remark, that if the multiplication of man's power over brute matter were so great as you suppose it to be, it could have no effect in the increasing difficulty of procuring food, except to the partial extent I have mentioned ; and that its influence, even in cheapening manufactures, must be determined by a very different formula from that you have adopted. By far the largest portion of labor-saving machines have no appreciable effect whatever on the price of manufactures, and many of the residue tend rather to prevent the rise of price than actually to lower it—as those in coal mines, &c. The prices of hardware and cutlery are, perhaps, about half what they were a century ago. Linen fabrics are all cheaper, though to a less extent. Those of wool and silk are very little reduced in price. Coal, after having risen, has again fallen to its former price. In those of cotton the reduction has been incomparably the greatest. By the united effect of the inventions of the steam-engine, the spinning-jenny, the power-loom and Whitney's cotton-gin, probably 8 yards of cotton cloth may now be bought for the same price which one yard would have cost sixty years since; and the cotton manufactures give employment, perhaps, to one-third of the whole manufacturing labor of Great Britain, and constitute more than half the exports. Let us now apply the touchstone of experience, to see how all this saving of labor, which, reduced as it is below your estimates, all will admit to be prodigious, affects the condition of the laborer. He can now for a day's work buy more and better shirts, &c., and his wife and daughters may wear more and better gowns and petticoats. Many other little comforts are also more attainable ; but as to the far more important matter of food, the same day's work will earn him a smaller number of pounds of bread or meat :* from which it would appear that whatever effect the progress of the useful and unclassical arts may have had in augmenting the quantity of food, whether by improvements in husbandry or by means of foreign commerce, that effect has been neutralized, and more than neutralized, by an increase of population.

In short, sir, the supposition that the *real* wages of labor, estimated in provisions, will increase with the increase of population, seems to me pretty much the same as to suppose that the price of bread will fall in a besieged town : the only difference between the two cases being, that in one the price rises in consequence of an increased demand, and in the other of a diminished supply. And if, in the one case, some few countries, under peculiar circum-

stances, like the United States, may experience no fall of wages with the increase of population, or, in the other case, an individual may here and there, by extraordinary efforts and address, make his earnings keep pace with the gradual rise of bread, these rare exceptions must be regarded but as temporary, and, sooner or later, they must obey the general law.

It is now, I fear, but too apparent that, in this discussion, we, by a common infirmity, are contending for victory as well as truth ; and it is equally apparent that many an arrow, as good as those already used, still lurks in our quivers, by reason of which the controversy, even now so far exceeding what either of us first expected, may be interminably protracted. To avoid so inconvenient a result, what do you say to our agreeing that either may put an end to it whenever he thinks proper, by publishing our correspondence ? In that event, the " impartial public," as we must now call it, in forming its conclusions, may admit, perhaps, that we know something of the subject : and though it should deny us this praise, it cannot fail to give us credit for good temper and civility in our disputation, as well as for constancy of purpose.

You will soon have an excellent opportunity of bringing your theory to the test of observation and experience. According to that theory, wages ought to be higher in China than in any other country in the world. It is equal to any other in the industry and manual skill of its people, and it exceeds all others in density ; yet, if I have been rightly informed, the minimum rate of wages there are not, as in every part of Europe, enough to support a family, but barely enough to support the individual laborer. But, you will say, they have no steam-engines and spinning-jennies, and they do not import provisions. That is true ; but what effect could labor-saving machines have in saving them from the necessity of eating dead cats, for want of better food ? Or how could they lessen the number of those who are now willing to do a day's work for less than a good meal ? And what would importation avail towards feeding 300 millions of people ? That country must, at all events, afford abundant materials for illustrating our subject ; and though I risk your there obtaining farther arguments to refute or to puzzle me, I cordially wish you a safe arrival in the Celestial Empire, and a pleasant and profitable residence there.

With sentiments of friendship and respect, I am, &c. &c.,

(Signed,) GEORGE TUCKER.

Hon. A. H. Everett.

NO. VIII.

Mr. Everett to Professor Tucker,

New York, May 25, 1845.

DEAR SIR,—I received, since my arrival here from Boston a few days ago, your letter of the 28th ult. I shall embark in a day or two for China, and am now entirely occupied in preparing for the expedition. During our three months' voyage I shall have ample leisure for correspondence, and I will prepare an answer on board the Columbus, which I may, perhaps, send from some port where we may touch on our way to the Celestial Empire.

In the meantime, I remain, dear sir, very truly, your friend and obedient servant,

(Signed,) A. H. EVERETT.

Hon. Geo. Tucker.

NO. IX.

Mr. Everett to Professor Tucker.

On board the U. S. Ship Columbus,
July 16, 1845.

DEAR SIR—Agreeably to my promise, in my note from New York, I avail myself of the leisure afforded by my present position to make a few comments upon your last letter.

Permit me to assure you that it was not from want of attention to the preceding one that I did not take up in detail all the points upon which you touch. I read the letter with great care several times—once aloud to a friend, with whom I conversed fully upon every suggestion. If I did not attend to them all in my reply, it was not because I thought any of them unimportant, but because I considered some of them, though in themselves valuable and interesting, as not bearing directly upon the question we have been discussing.

I concur with you in the opinion that after an improvement has taken place in the productiveness of manufacturing la-

bor, the price of the product gradually falls abroad as well as at home. I had previously remarked in my answer to your first letter, that competition soon reduces the profits in this branch of trade to the ordinary level. At this point it is regularly carried on. The articles exchanged are furnished on both sides at the cost of production with the usual profit. The importer advances the cost of transportation and the duty, if there be one, adding them with his own profit, to the price at which he purchases the article. to the retail dealer, who in turn, sells it at this price, with his own profit added, to the consumer. The advantage obtained by the community, in which the increase of population has taken place, consists in getting their manufactures at much lower rates than before, and their food at the cheapest rate at which it can be raised in the best soils, with the necessary addition for the cost of transportation.

In regard to the operation of the cost of transporting provisions from a distance upon the trade, which has been one of the principal points in discussion between us, you adhere in your last letter to the suggestion made in the preceding one, that the case of provisions forms in this respect a sort of exception to the usual course of the laws of trade, according to which the value of articles at the place where they are wanted, is in general determined by the cost of transportation and production; and the only effect of increasing the cost of transportation is to make an equivalent addition to the price paid by the consumer. You appear to think that these rules do not operate in the usual way in the case of provisions for the reason that human food is consumed in - producing and transporting food. Concurring with you in the correctness of this last suggestion, I must say that I am not able to perceive how the case of provisions differs in this respect from that of any other article. The subsistence of the producer and carrier is one of the regular elements in the price of every product of labor. If we suppose, as you appear to do, in the cases you state by way of illustration, that the carrier takes the provisions intended for his own use with him, and that they completely fill his carriage, he will, of course, have none left to sell at his place of destination.

But the same would be true of a trade in any other article. If the food intended for the carrier occupy the whole of the carriage, he can no more carry broadcloth or hardware than Indian corn. On this point I can only repeat what I have said in a preceding letter, that the cost of production and transportation, however high it may be, will not prevent the prosecution of the trade, so long as the consumer is able and willing to purchase the article at the enhanced price. Your idea, if I rightly understand you, is, that when the subsistence of the carrier is equal to the cost of producing the article, the trade ceases. But there are numerous cases in which the cost of transportation, including, of course, the subsistence of the carrier, and the duty, far exceeds the cost of production. The duty now imposed at Havana upon flour imported in American vessels, which is ten dollars the barrel, is double the cost of production. The duty imposed in England upon the importation of good Virginia staple tobacco, amounts to several hundred per cent. upon the cost of production. The only question in regard to the practicability of a particular branch of trade is, whether it will pay the ordinary mercantile profit. If it will not, it must be abandoned. If it will, it will be continued whatever may be the proportion which the cost of transportation bears to that of production.

You appear to think that I have greatly overrated the extent of the improvements in the productiveness of manufacturing labor in Great Britain, and state particularly that your own estimate is considerably lower than mine. This remark must have been made inadvertently, for you will find, on recurring to my letter, that your estimate, though much lower than some others that I allude to is a good deal higher than the one that I assume for the present purpose. After remarking that some persons have estimated this improvement at three thousand per cent., and others at eight thousand, I assume for practical use the calculation of one hundred. You say that the best judges consider the improvement as equivalent to the labor of from twenty to twenty-five millions of men. This upon a working population of from eight to ten millions, is equivalent to an addition of from two to three hundred per cent. to the productiveness of the labor of the

community, which is double or triple the amount that I assume.

Although your estimate is two or three times as high as mine, which I purposely reduced to the lowest point in order to preclude the possibility of mistake or cavil, I must add, that I have met with no calculation which brings down the extent of improvements in manufacturing labor so low as you do, in estimating them as equivalent to an addition of only from twenty to twenty-five millions of men. Mr. John Quincy Adams, who, from his familiarity with the state of England, and with political inquiries in general, must be regarded as a highly respectable authority, represents them in one of his speeches in Congress as equivalent to the labor of three hundred millions. Robert Owen assumes eight hundred; and although his political theories may be often visionary, there is probably no man living better acquainted with the statistical details of the state of manufacturing labor in his own country. It is unnecessary, however, for me to enlarge upon this point in defence of the position taken in my preceding letters, where, in order to be entirely on the safe side, I have, as I remarked before, assumed, the very low estimate of only eight or ten millions.

You intimate that the correspondence between us seems to have reached its natural termination, and in that I agree with you. I am not concious of having been influenced in commencing or conducting it by a mere desire of victory, that is, of convincing you of the correctness of my opinions. I am well aware that the usual effect of all controversy is to strengthen each party in his own views. In your address to the Institute, you assumed as an acknowledged principle in political economy, that wages must fall in this country with the progress of population, without stating your reason for entertaining this idea. I have for many years past felt a strong interest in the question of the effect of the progress of population upon the supply of the means of subsistence, and the general reward of labor, considering it as the leading one in the science, and as lying at the bottom of the various plans for social reform, that successively agitate the community. Regarding you as one of the highest authorities in the country upon a question on political philosophy, I was anxious to learn whether your reasons for entertaining opinions alluded to were peculiar to the yourself, or were the same with those of the British disciples of the school of Malthus ; and it was for the purpose of informing myself upon this point that I took the liberty of writing to you. Your first letter gave me the information that I sought ; and I should not have troubled you with any comments upon the points on which we differ, had you not particularly requested me to do so.

Agreeing with me in the opinion that the progress of population is naturally attended with a positive increase in the productiveness of both manufacturing and agricultural labor, you apprehend a decline in the rate of wages from the effect of a deficiency in the supply of food, which you suppose to be another result of the same cause. A deficiency of this kind in the supply of food or any other article, of course corrects itself, so far as this can be done by the regular operation of the laws of trade ; and there is no apparent reason why provisions, if deficient, may not be introduced by sea or land, to any extent, at any point where they are wanted, excepting the cost of the operation, or a deficiency in the supply abroad. The question, how far, if at all, these causes would prevent in this case the regular course of the laws of trade, is accordingly the point upon which the discussion between us has mainly turned, and which I have supposed to be the only material one. You have stated your reasons for believing that the cost of transporting provisions from a distance is too great to permit the existence of the trade to any considerable extent, and also that the supply from abroad must always, from the nature of the case, be much too limited to cover the supposed deficiency. I have endeavored to show that in the case of a deficiency of provisions of native origin, resulting from the progress of population, the trade in the foreign article must necessarily be profitable to any extent to which a supply may be wanted, and that there is no necessary limit to the amount of this supply short of the exhaustion of the whole productive power of the globe. I stated briefly but distinctly upon these points all that I think material,

and I suppose that you have done the same. The decision of the question must depend upon the comparative value of our argument, in regard to which other persons are, of course, better judges than I am. I have never considered the correspondence as confidential, and am quite willing that you should, as you appear inclined to do, take the opinion of your friends, or the public, upon it in any way that you may deem expedient. My friend, Mr. O'Sullivan, to whom I have communicated a part of the correspondence, expressed a wish to publish it, when complete, in the *Democratic Review.* I shall send him a copy for this purpose by the same conveyance that takes this letter.

You remark that I shall have an opportunity, in China, of testing the correctness of the principles that I have stated in these letters, and appear to suppose that the experience of that country rather tends to disprove them. Without anticipating what may be the result of my own observations, which I shall be most happy, as you suggest, to communicate to you, I will add here a few hints from a writer, whose work I happen to be now reading for a different purpose, and who considers China as affording the strongest example of the beneficial effect of the progress of population upon the welfare of nations. The book is a recent publication, entitled " The Chinese as they are," by Mr. Tradescent Lay, a British missionary, and apparently a judicious and careful observer.

" The prosperity of the Chinese tempts one to frame a system of political economy which lays population as the foundation whereon everything in the way of social comfort or personal affluence is reared. The wealth of the community grows out of men, and not out of the soil, excepting in a secondary and subordinate sense. I look upon man as the great capital of a nation—a view which is based upon what I see in China, where a swarming people are encircled by a swarm of comforts. In no country do the inhabitants crowd every habitable spot as in China ; and in no country do the poor people abound with so many of the elegancies and luxuries of life. In China the shops overflow with everything that can attract the eye or provoke the appetite— all under the more effectual lure of a low price. A native is thus stirred up to industrious habits, not by the iron hand of compulsion, but by the charming hopes of enjoyment. The worth of his money engenders frugality, and thus adds a sister grace to industry. The ease with which a family may be maintained, nerves him to indulge the love of matrimony, and he lays by something to purchase a house, with a beautiful wife to adorn it. Early marriage encourages fertility, and augments the population already vast, and consequently the means of living, which bear a ratio to the population. Thus we are carried round in a circle, and brought back to man, with the benediction—'Increase and multiply and replenish the earth,' as the corner stone of national prosperity.

"In China the natives throng all those parts which are susceptible of tillage, till there is not room enough to hold them, and we find at the same time a supply of comforts for the poor such as no other country can parallel. It is a favorite theorem with some, that while the population goes on increasing in geometrical progression, the products of the soil, or rather the means of subsistence increase only in the arithmetical. In China the luxuries of life have also increased in the same geometrical ratio; and in other parts of the world they will be found to have followed the same law, when proper allowance is made for circumstances. When the corn-laws and other enactments that have sprung out of the same stingy, short-sighted policy shall have been repealed, and foreigners shall be allowed to sell us their produce freely, the welfare of our poor will increase with their numbers. They owe their present unfortunate predicament to legislation ; and they will commence a new era in their happiness, when the unstatesmanlike practice of taking from one part of the community and given to another shall have been forgotten."

We are now twelve days out, and have had thus far a most prosperous voyage, not having yet experienced a single day of bad weather, calm or head wind. We already feel the first breathings of the north-easterly trade winds, upon which we calculate to waft us to the vicinity of the line. Our ship sails magnificently, though not permitted to develope her full capacity by the slower movement of her consort, the Vincennes. I often think how the noble old discoverer would have exulted to have had the command of such a squadron for his great expedition.

Our first port will be Rio, whence I expect to despatch this letter. With many thanks for your kind wishes, and in the hopes of hearing from you while abroad, I remain, dear sir, very truly and respectfully your friend,
A. H. EVERETT.

Hon. Geo. Tucker.

THE

UNITED STATES MAGAZINE,

AND

DEMOCRATIC REVIEW.

Vol. XXI.   NOVEMBER, 1847.   No. CXIII.

THE CONDITION OF CHINA,

WITH REFERENCE TO THE MALTHUSIAN THEORY, AS DISCUSSED IN A CORRE-
SPONDENCE BETWEEN ALEX. H. EVERETT AND PROF. GEO. TUCKER, LATE
OF THE UNIVERSITY OF VIRGINIA.

MACAO, *April* 30, 1847.

DEAR SIR,—

In a letter, which I addressed to you, nearly a year ago, from on board the United States ship Columbus, I promised to communicate to you the result of my observations on the state of population in this country, and its influence upon the reward of labor, or rate of wages—a question which had previously been the subject of an amicable correspondence between us. I quoted in that letter a passage from a recent work by Mr. Tradescant Say, in which he expressed the opinion, that the condition of the mass of the people in China affords a remarkable example of the favorable influence of the density of population upon the supply of the necessaries and comforts of life ; and would even authorise the belief, which he professed himself to entertain, that the progress of population is the true index and principal immediate cause of the progress of national prosperity.

I regret to be obliged to add, that this estimable person, who, after publishing the work alluded to, was appointed British Consul at Amoy,—one of the four newly-opened ports,—has since died at his post. He was highly esteemed by his countrymen, and by the foreign community in general, and his early death is deplored as a public loss. He was one of the few foreigners who were willing to pardon some peculiarities of manners and character in the inhabitants of the Celestial Empire ; and, without overlooking their defects, to render justice to their good qualities. It has given me pleasure to be able to cite the authority of so competent a judge in support of my own views, and, at the same time, to pay this slight tribute of respect to the memory of a most deserving and excellent man.

The state of the population in China is, on every account, a very curious subject. Its immense and wholly unparalleled amount—supposing the commonly received accounts to be well established—renders it one of the moral wonders of the world. Nearly four hundred millions of men, associated under one government, and composing one consolidated state—are a phenomenon, not only unequalled, but entirely unapproached in political history. It becomes, therefore, a matter of great interest to ascertain, first, how far the commonly received accounts can be relied on,—in other words, what the population of China really is ;—and, secondly, what sort of influence it exercises upon the character and condition of the people. So far as I have had opportunity to examine the subject, I see no reason to reject the common accounts, in which I also understand you to concur. The wonder, in fact, does not lie so much in the great density of the population, since China, in this respect, does not differ materially from the more densely peopled portions of Europe. It lies rather in the vast number of persons, who are here congregated into one political system. In regard to the influence of the state of population, such as it is, you suppose that its extraordinary density has had a disastrous operation upon the condition of the working classes, and reduced them to abject misery. I think I shall be able to satisfy you that this opinion is erroneous, and that the working classes in China are fully as well, if not better paid for their labor than those of any other country.

1 will, first, however, make a few remarks upon the real amount of the population, in confirmation of the statements that are now generally received.

The statements of the population of this empire, which have long been before the public, rest in official enumerations, regularly taken, or corrected, every year. The whole empire is divided for administrative purposes into provinces, and these, again, into departments and smaller districts, the lowest of which are composed of ten families—all, from the province to the decade, having their appropriate heads. The head of each district of ten families is required to keep a tablet, upon which is entered the number of the persons in each of the families composing his district, under the two general heads of able-bodied men, or *tax-payers*, and *mouths*—or women and children. Once in every year the governor of each province collects these tablets and makes a return of the population, founded upon them, to the Board of Revenue or Treasury Department, at Peking. Here they are put in order and employed for the various purposes, such as military service, taxation, &c., for which such a return is wanted. The result is published from time to time, by authority, and thus possesses all the certainty that can well belong to the subject.

Sir George Staunton, in his account of the embassy of Lord Macartney, gives a statement of the total population of China, and of that of each of the provinces, taken for him from these returns by *Shoo-Ta-Gin*—a Mandarin of high standing and character. The total is three hundred and thirty-three millions. The amount for each province is also given in round numbers. It is apparent from this circumstance, that precise accuracy was not arrived at; but I know no reason for supposing that the number of millions was not in each case accurately taken.

Another statement, founded on the same returns, as made at a more recent period, was first published in the *Companion to the Anglo-Chinese Calendar*, for the year 1832, and has since been generally adopted as the most authentic account of the actual population of China. It purports to give the returns, made up for the seventeenth year of the Emperor Kia-King— 1812—as published by authority in the *Ta-Tsing-Hoog-Teen*, an Imperial Statute Book, at Peking, in the year 1828. It gives in exact numbers the amount for each province, and the total for the whole empire. The latter is 360,279,897. The population of the province of Canton, according to that estimate, is 19,174,030, or about the same with the present population of the whole United States.

As the population appears to have been increasing with rapidity ever since the accession of the now reigning dynasty, about two centuries ago, and as there is an interval of twenty years between the date of this return and that of the one given to Lord Macartney, the difference between them may be accounted for very naturally by the intervening increase. These two statements, therefore, agree very well together. That of 1812 is, of course, preferable from the greater accuracy with which the numbers are given.

The same returns, upon which this statement is founded, are contained in fuller detail in a publication of the distinguished French orientalist, M. Pauthier, entitled, " *Documens Statistiques et Officielles sur l'Empire de la Chine, traduits du Chinois, par G. Pauthier, Paris*, 1841." " Statistical and official documents respecting the Chinese Empire, translated from the Chinese." This is an exact translation from the Chinese official publication, alluded to above, entitled, *Ta-Tsing-Hoog-Teen*, or the " Imperial Statute Book." The copy, employed by Pauthier, belongs to the Royal Library at Paris, and, although the date of the edition is not given in the title-page, includes documents of later date than 1812. The work is a complete statement, by authority, of the population, the revenue and the distribution of the land throughout the whole empire— interspersed with explanations of the manner in which the returns are made.   In regard to population we have the following particulars :

> "In each section, the person who has charge of the enumeration of the inhabitants, shall provide himself with tablets, one of which is to be hung up at the door of each house.   On this shall be written the name of the head of the family, with those of the able-bodied men, or tax-payers, and of the women and children.   The list shall be examined every year, in order to make the necessary changes.   In the tenth moon of each year the Governors of provinces shall send round and collect from the *Pao-Kias*, or heads of ten families, these tablets.   An abstract of these, with a calculation of the revenue resulting from it shall be transmitted to the Board of Revenue at Peking, where it shall form the basis of the annual report upon the finances and revenue of the empire."

The work of Pauthier, from which I make these extracts, and which is a pamphlet of fifty pages, includes a large portion of the returns for 1812 in detail.   For the present purpose, I need only say, farther, that it gives, as the report of the total amount of the population for that year, 361,693,177. There is a slight difference between this result and the one deduced from the same returns in the Anglo-Chinese Calendar.   It is accounted for by the admission into the statement, as given by Pauthier, of two or three smaller items, which I need not here specify.

This is a far more carefully made up, and consequently more *reliable* estimate of the population of China, than we have of any other country on the globe, with, perhaps, the exception of the United States.   We may, therefore, with safety, assume it as correct, especially as for the principal purpose which we have in view,—I mean the influence of the state of the population upon the condition of the people ;—the total amount is of no material consequence—the result in this respect depending entirely upon the comparative density, and not the positive numbers.

This immense population appears to be of somewhat recent growth.   The most ancient return, that I have seen, dates from the 26th year of Hoong-Woo,—1393 of our era.   In this the number of families is stated at 16,052,860, and that of individuals at 60,545,811.   The next authentic statement is the return of tax-payers for the 50th year of Kang-Hee,—1712 of our era.   The number is stated at 29,642,492.   Multiplying this number by five, we have a total of 145,000,000 for the whole population of the empire.   This is the estimate of Father Amyot, one of the most distinguished of the French Jesuits, given in a work published by him about the middle of the last century.   Supposing it to be correct for the time to which it is referred,—1712,—the population doubled itself between that period and the year 1794, when Lord Macartney visited Peking.   Between this latter date and 1812, it must have increased about thirty millions.

It is remarkable, however, that the Emperor Keen-Loong, in a proclamation addressed to the people at large upon the very subject of the population, and published in the work before quoted, *Ta-Tsing-Hoog-teen*, or "Imperial Statute Book," sec. 141, p. 38—states that, in the 49th year of Kang-Hee, the population of the empire was 23,312,200.   "Last year," he adds, "the amount, according to returns, made from all the provinces, was 307,467,200."   This proclamation was published by Keen-Loong in the 53d year of his reign,—1794,—the year before Lord Macartney's embassy ; so it is not easy to reconcile the Emperor's statement for that year with the one of 330 millions given to Lord Macartney by *Thoo-ta-gin ;* but the difficulty is greatly increased, when we find the Emperor representing the whole population for the 49th year of Kang-Hee,—1712,—at only 23 millions. On this supposition it must have sunk between the years 1393 and 1712, from sixty to twenty-three millions; and then, in the next eighty years, suddenly started forward from 23 millions to 307. The conquest of the empire by the Manchoo Tartars,—the now reigning dynasty,—took place between the reigns of Hoong-Woo and Kang Hee,—say about the year 1650,—and was attended by long and bloody wars, that, no doubt, produced at this time a considerable effect upon the population; but such alternations of decline and progress, as are suggested by the statements given in the Emperor's proclamation, appear to be wholly inadmissible. The most natural, and probably the true way of accounting for the apparent difficulty, is to suppose that the Emperor inadvertently described as a return of the whole population, what was intended, and is, in fact, described in other official publications, as a return of tax-payers only. Considered in this light, and multiplying the number it gives by five, it serves, as I have already said, for the basis of an estimate of about 145 millions,—which agrees very well with the more recent accounts. Unfortunately for this hypothesis, the Emperor himself affirms, in the same proclamation, that "between the 49th year of Kang-Hee and the time when he wrote, the population of the empire had increased about *fifteen-fold*," and expresses some alarm as to the possibility of finding subsistence for the people, should their numbers continue to advance in the same proportion. Indeed, the principal object of the proclamation is to enjoin great industry in raising food, and great economy in the use of it, on the assumed ground, that the population was rapidly outstripping the means of subsistence. It is apparent, therefore, that the Emperor Keen-Loong really supposed the return of twenty-three millions for the year 1712, to be a return of the whole individual population of the empire. It is difficult to imagine how a sovereign of eminent talent and high literary accomplishments, like Keen-Loong, should have fallen into this error. Possibly a more careful examination of the original may discover some mistake in the translation, which may enable us to explain the mystery. In the meantime, as it has no bearing upon the evidence in support of the official returns, there is no reason why it should make us doubt the accuracy of the estimate founded upon them, and now generally received as authentic and certain.

We may, therefore, as I remarked before, assume with safety for the present purpose, that the total population of the Chinese Empire amounts, in round numbers, to about three hundred and seventy millions. This immense mass is distributed in different degrees of density over a territory, the extent of which has been variously stated. Mr. J. Q. Adams, in his lecture on China, reckons it in round numbers at seven millions of square miles,—including, of course, Chinese Tartary;—Balbi, perhaps the highest authority, and who, in this case, has the endorsement of Humboldt, states it at 5,350,000. This would give, for the whole empire, a density of about seventy to the square mile. Much the greater part of the population is, however, concentrated in China proper, which includes 1,297,000 square miles, or 836,719,630 English acres. On that territory the population stands to the geographical extent in the ratio of 257 to the square mile. This is not higher than the average ratio in the thickly-peopled parts of Europe. In some parts of the Netherlands, for example, the ratio is 275; in England, about 225; in the Grand-duchy of Lucca, 250. In the province of Yoonnan, in China proper, the average is as low as 74, which is rather lower than it is in the state of Massachusetts; while in Chee-Lee, the most populous of all, and the one which includes Peking, the average rises to 644. In the province of Kwantung (Canton) it is stated at 264.

I need hardly say that the influence of the state of population upon the condition of the people is determined entirely by its density, and not by the amount that may happen to be incorporated into one political system. The state of population in China, considered as a fact to be studied and accounted for, belongs, therefore, to the same class with the state of population in the thickly-peopled parts of Europe,—such as England, Switzerland, the Netherlands, and the north of Italy.

The theory on the subject of the relation naturally subsisting between the state of population and the supply of the means of subsistence, which has of late prevailed in Great Britain, and which you have adopted as applicable to the United States, undertakes to prove that the reward of labor, or rate of wages, regularly declined in proportion to the increase of density in the population. You intimate, in one of your letters to me, that I shall find the truth of this principle confirmed by the existing state of things in China : in other words, that the reward of labor is lower, and the mass of the people consequently in a less comfortable situation than in other less densely peopled countries.

The impression that I have received from my reading upon the subject, as well as from such personal observations as I have been able to make, is different ; and I think I shall be able to satisfy you, that, although the money price of labor, as of most other articles, is lower here than it is in the United Sates, the real rate of wages,—that is, the supply of the necessaries and comforts of life, which the laborer is able to procure with his pay, is greater than it is in most other countries, including those which we regard as the best administered and most prosperous in the western world.

In the remarks which you make upon the subject, in your letter, you do not go into any detailed statements of the grounds of your opinion in regard to the situation of the working class in China. You would, perhaps, rely, in some degree, upon the authority of Malthus, who takes the same view of the matter that you do,—and upon the evidence, adduced in support of it, in his Essay on Population.

" The reward of labor in China, (he remarks,) is kept as low as possible, and the mass of the people are in the most abject state of poverty. The price of labor is generally found to bear as small a proportion everywhere to the rate demanded for provisions, as the common people can suffer. Notwithstanding the advantage of living together in large families. like soldiers in a mess, and the exercise of the greatest economy in the management of these messes, they are reduced to the use of vegetable food, with a very rare and scanty relish of any animal substance."

These statements are given by Malthus on the authority of Sir George Staunton. He adds, on that of Du Halde, that, " notwithstanding the great sobriety and industry of the inhabitants, the prodigious number of them occasions a great deal of misery. There are some so poor, that, being unable to supply their children with common necessaries, they expose them in the streets. In the great cities, such as Canton and Peking, this shocking sight is very common."

He farther adds, on the authority of Father Premare, one of the Jesuit missionaries, writing to a friend, that—

" The richest and most flourishing empire in the world is, notwithstanding, in one sense, the poorest and most miserable of all. The country, however extensive and fertile, is not sufficient to support its inhabitants. *Four times as much territory would be necessary to place them at their ease.* In Canton alone, there is, without exaggeration, more than a million of souls; and in a town, three or four miles distant, (Foo-Shaw,) a still greater number. Who, then, can count the inhabitants of the province ? But what is this to the whole empire, which contains fifteen great provinces, all equally peopled ? To how many millions would such a calculation amount ? *A third part of this infinite population would hardly find sufficient rice to support itself properly.*

" It is well known that extreme misery impels a people to the most dreadful excesses.

A spectator in China, who examines things closely, will not be surprised, that mothers destroy, or expose many of their children,—that parents sell their daughters for a trifle,—that the people are selfish, and that there are such numbers of robbers. The surprise is, that nothing still more dreadful should happen; and that in times of famine, which are here but too frequent, millions of people should perish with hunger, without having recourse to those dreadful extremities of which we read examples in the history of Europe.

"It cannot be said, in China, as in Europe, that the poor are idle, and might gain a subsistence if they would work. The labors and efforts of these people are beyond conception. A Chinese will pass whole days in digging the earth,—sometimes up to the knees in water,—*and in the evening, is happy to eat a little spoonful of rice, and to drink the insipid water in which it was boiled. This is all that they have in general.*"

These are the principal authorities cited by Malthus in support of his assertions in regard to the supposed "abject poverty" of the mass of the people, and the "extreme smallness" of the reward of their labor, as compared with what it is in other countries.

As respects the supposed practice of exposing infant children, alluded to in the above extract and elsewhere, as one of the evidences of the very wretched state of the working classes in China, I cannot, of course, go into detail in the short compass of a letter. There is reason to believe, that in some of the statements made upon this subject, the truth has been greatly exaggerated, and that the crime in question is not more frequent than it is in the more populous parts of the Christian world,—particularly in some of the great cities of the continent of Europe. If the view which I take of the state of the people be correct, it must be attributed, when it does occur, to the same causes which produce it elsewhere, viz., in shame, or sheer profligacy, and not to an extremity of destitution, which, as I shall presently show, is itself entirely imaginary.

Before entering into particulars, I will remark, in the first place, that the density of population—even taking into view only China proper—is not greater, as I have shown, than it is in the thickly-peopled parts of Europe. If this supposed wretchedness of the mass of the people be real, and be, also, the effect of the density of the population, how happens it that it does not exist in England, the Netherlands, Switzerland, and the north of Italy—countries, in which the population is of about the same density as in China, and which are, by general acknowledgment, precisely the most prosperous and flourishing parts of Europe? It is obvious, that the wretchedness supposed is either imaginary and unreal, or that, so far as it may be real, it is the effect of some other cause, since the same density of population, existing in other countries, not only does not produce this effect, but coincides with the most remarkable developments of national prosperity that are recorded in the history of the world.

Again : we are told by Father Premare, in the extract given above, that "there is not rice enough grown to support one-third of the population ;"—yet rice, we know, is the main article of food. What, then, becomes of the other two-thirds? It is obvious, that, if this assertion were true, it would take but one or two years to reduce the population to a third of the present amount. This remark is sufficient of itself to show the degree of attention which is due to the statements of the worthy father, considered as *scientific data.* He was a person of superior talent and excellent character, and, withal, a very good writer ;—large portions of his correspondence, as given in the *Lettres Curieuses et Edificantes,* in which the letter here quoted is contained, are very interesting. But he evidently wrote, on this occasion, with no view to scientific accuracy, and really means nothing more than that the Empire of China was very populous, and that he had reason to believe, that there was, at times, a great deal of suffering among the poor.

Even this immense disproportion between the supply of food and the number of mouths does not satisfy the worthy father, who, after stating that there is not rice enough raised to support more than a third of the people, remarks, as you have seen, in another part of the same passage, that there is not territory enough to furnish food for more than a quarter. " *Four times as much territory would be necessary to place the people at their ease.*"— Now, the extent of the territory of China, including Chinese Tartary, is reckoned by the best geographers, as I have already stated, at 5,350,000 square miles. The portion of the earth's surface, available for agricultural purposes, is about twenty million square miles. Four times the territory of China would be equal to the whole surface of the earth, so far as it is susceptible of cultivation. According to the statement of Father Premare, therefore, it would require the whole possible produce of the globe to supply with food the population of the Empire of China, which, when he wrote, amounted to about a hundred and fifty millions. Truly, the Jesuit, if he calculated their appetites upon his own, must have been, like Shylock's attendant in the play, a " huge feeder." It is estimated that in England, which is not a productive country, an acre laid down in wheat will supply more than enough for the food of two men,—laid down in potatoes, it will furnish food for six. As rice is one of the most productive articles that can be raised, and as, in China, two crops are regularly gathered every year from the same land, it would be fair to take a higher number than six, as that of the men who can be supported in China by the produce of an acre : but assuming the same ratio for the sake of moderation, and reckoning the five million square miles of territory at four thousand million English acres, we shall have, multiplying these by six, twenty-four thousand millions as the number of men who might be supported by the produce of the present territory of China, if it were all under cultivation. There is, therefore, even now, when the population is about triple what it was in the time of Premare, " ample room to raise enough" for a still larger addition. Four times the territory of China, on the same calculation, would feed about a hundred thousand millions of men.

So much for the scientific value of Father Premare's observations in political economy. The general considerations that I have now presented might, perhaps, be sufficient of themselves to refute statements resting upon so little evidence, and carrying with them such decisive internal proof of inaccuracy—not to say the wildest jumping in the dark. But the real test of truth is, after all, an appeal to facts. Are the mass of the people in China in the state of abject wretchedness here supposed, or are they not? Is the reward of labor barely sufficient to keep soul and body together? or is it, at least, equal to what it is in the most prosperous and flourishing communities in Christendom? It is rather remarkable, that neither the present missionaries, who have given their appalling accounts of the misery of the people, nor their modern British disciples, have thought it worth while to inform themselves as to what the rate of wages, and the cost of the necessaries of life, really are. A few facts of this kind would elucidate the subject more than whole volumes of mere speculation.

The average rate of wages paid to the daily laborer is the most correct index that we can have of the average reward of mere labor in all its branches, taken independently of skill in every other extraneous circumstance. The wages usually paid to domestic servants in China are five dollars a month. I am also informed on good authority, and find it stated in a well-written article in the *Chinese Repository*, now before me, that the wages paid to servants by foreigners here, are about the same with those which they receive from their own countrymen. It appears, from the same authority, that the wages of a laborer in the field or the workshop, are generally one *mace* a day. Porters, menials, and other mere laborers, get about the same. One *mace* a day may, therefore, be assumed as the average rate of the reward of mere daily labor in China. A *mace* is the tenth part of a *tael*, and about the seventh part of a Spanish dollar, or from fourteen to fifteen cents.

Persons of the description here mentioned can be boarded at from a dollar to a dollar and a half a month. Mine are boarded at $1.50. Their food, as thus provided, is not, as Father Premare describes that of the poor Chinese in general, " a little spoonful of rice," nor their drink, the "insipid water in which it was boiled." They have for their $1.50 the month, as much rice as they can eat three times a day. This is the great staple of food with all classes, from the Emperor downwards. In addition to this, they have fish, fowls, and pork in abundance : beef and mutton are scarce and dear. They have also an ample supply of vegetables and fruits— such as oranges and bananas. For drink, they have tea at discretion at all hours. This is the universal beverage throughout the empire.

I may add here, that the worthy Father Premare, who has rendered important services to Chinese literature by his excellent Grammar, but who is naturally not so much at home in the kitchen as he is in the library, has made a rather amusing mistake in regard to this matter of "the water in which the rice is boiled." The Chinese, who are very particular in preparing their rice, employ but little water in boiling it ; and permit the whole to evaporate before they consider the rice as fit for use. The rice, when served, is perfectly dry; each kernel is entirely separate from the rest, and "the insipid water in which it was boiled," has all gone off in vapor. Famine-struck, as Father Premare supposes him to be, the poorest Chinese would not touch a dish of rice which should have left behind it in the vessel in which it was boiled, this "insipid potation," although a similar mess is daily consumed with infinite relish throughout our well-fed and luxurious New-England. At the South they understand the matter better, and boil their rice as well as the Chinese.

I mentioned above that good, common board may be had at from one to one dollar fifty the month. As an instance of the former rate, Mr. Brown, a missionary clergyman, who keeps a school for Chinese boys at Hong-Kong, in which there are from twenty to thirty pupils, boards them at the rate of a dollar a month, in the manner described above.

The average cost of rice is about one and a half taels the pearl, ($133\frac{1}{3}$ lbs.,) or a cent a pound; and a pound of rice is as much as a man can eat in a day. The daily laborer receives, therefore, in his *mace*, an amount of money equivalent in value to the daily subsistence of fourteen or fifteen men. If he be the head of a family, comprised of four or five persons, he has at his disposal, after providing for his and their subsistence, the means of subsistence for nine or ten persons, to be employed in providing himself and his family with clothes, lodging, books and other necessaries and comforts. These are all to be had at the most moderate rates. " A common laborer," says the authority, I just quoted, "can live for $2.25 a month, including clothes and rent ; but $3 is probably nearer the average. Cotton clothing costs from $4 to $5 a year." The people, as I have already remarked, are very much in the habit of living together in large establishments, composed of several branches of the same family. In consequence of this truly admirable system, which combines all the supposed advantages of the visionary scheme of " communities," without any of its dangers and absurdities, the expenses of individuals are greatly reduced. " Eight, twelve fifteen, forty, and even sixty persons," says the authority I have already quoted, " sometimes live in one house. This, of course, reduces the individual expenses; and this practice is so common, that $2.50 may be taken as the average rate of b ard." It is much to be wished, that this economical, social an l truly Christian custom might extend itself to other countries. It is constantly recommended to the Chinese by the highest authorities in the empire, and forms the subject of one of the chapters of the famous *Sacred Edict*, written by the Emperor Yoong-Ching, about a century ago—a sort of summary of political and social duty, which is read publicly every month by the provincial magistrates to assemblies of the people throughout the whole empire. In this, as well as in some other matters, to which I need not here allude, our philosophers, philanthropists, and even missionaries, might with advantage take a few lessons in political, moral and religious doctrine from the people whom they are so anxious to enlighten, and whom they consider as so far below themselves in the scale of civilization.

Such, however, are the facts in reference to the condition of the working classes in China. The account of a laborer of the lowest class with the world will stand, on an average, nearly as follows :

Annual income, at $5 the month,..	$60 00
Board, clothes and rent, at $2 25 the month,..	27 00
Surplus, to be employed in supporting a family, books, luxuries and savings,..........	$33 00

The correctness of the statements given is, for the most part, within my own knowledge ; and where they rest on evidence, the authority is unquestionable. You will judge for yourself how far they are consistent with the theory of " abject wretchedness." From a view of these statements, as well as of what I see around me, in the actual condition of the people, I should say on the contrary, that the working population of China are better fed, better clothed, better lodged, on the whole happier, and even higher in the scale of intellectual and moral culture, than, perhaps, any other on the globe. I doubt whether, even in New-England, where the money-price of labor is so much higher, either the laborer or the small cultivator enjoys so many of the comforts of life as the Chinese. Certainly the half-starved and over-worked wretches that crowd the factories, mines and work-houses of England, and pass from one to the other of these establishments with every oscillation in the ever-varying scale of prices, cannot pretend to an equality with him.

But without adverting to these less forward classes, although they compose more than half of the working population of England, and taking into view only the best paid and the best situated portion of the agricultural laborers, the proportion between the money price of their labor and the usual supply of the means of subsistence is far below what it is in China. The laborers on Sir Robert Peel's estate had their wages raised very recently from twelve to fifteen shillings a week, on account of the present scarcity. Their ordinary wages are twelve shillings, and the average reward of agricultural labor does not exceed ten, or £26 a year. A quarter of wheat is considered as the usual supply for the subsistence of an individual. This, at sixty shillings, or £3, absorbs about an eighth of his income, and leaving him but seven eighths for his family, clothing, rent, and other expenses ; while the personal subsistence of the labourer in China, absorbs, as we have seen, only one-fifteenth of his money wages. The comparative dearness of all the necessaries and comforts of life in England increases the difference still further. The tea which the Chinese laborer drinks from morning till night for next to nothing, pays in England a duty of a shilling a pound, in addition to the cost, and is, of course, beyond the reach of the poor. I cannot here pursue the subject into further details, but I trust that I have said enough to satisfy you beyond a doubt, of the truth of my general proposition, that the reward of labor in China is fully sufficient for the comfortable support of the laborer, and quite equal to what it is in the most prosperous communities of Europe and America.

The account given by Father Premare, in the above extract, of the condition of the working classes in China, though vague, and when analyzed, entirely without value for any scientific purpose, is yet fitted to leave a disagreeable impression upon the mind; and coming, as it does, from an intelligent eye-witness, can hardly fail, unless contrasted with other representations of the same kind, from equally good authority, to produce some effect. It forms, however, a sort of exception to the general character of the accounts given by the Jesuit missionaries; and I cannot help thinking it a little unfair in Mr. Malthus, to pick out those two or three passages from a large mass of matter contained in the same collection, almost the whole of which has a directly opposite tendency. Indeed, the disposition of the Jesuits to see everything here *en beau*, has been a standing topic of reproach against these worthy fathers; and, if their authority can be depended on, China must be regarded, not merely as a flourishing and prosperous community, but as a sort of earthly Elysium. At the risk of making my letter tedious, I will extract one or two passages of this kind, as an offset to the Jérémiade of Father Primare, who, inconsistently enough, in the midst of his lamentation over the "abject wretchedness" and "utter destitution" of the people, himself pronounces China to be the "most prosperous and flourishing community on the globe."

The following passage is taken from a letter from Father Fontaney to Father de la Chaise, the well-known confessor to Louis XIV. It describes the aspect of the country between Peking and Shen-See.

"The road from Peking to the province of Shen-See, is one of the most agreeable that I ever saw. You pass through nine or ten cities, and among others, that of *Pao-tim-foo*, the residence of the Viceroy. The whole country is level and well cultivated, the road smooth, and in many places bordered with trees, and with walls to protect and secure the fields. For the whole way there is a continual passing of men, carts, and beasts of burden. In the course of every league, you meet with two or three villages, not including those which you see at a distance from the road. The rivers are crossed by solid bridges of several arches. The most considerable of them is that of *Loo-Ko-Kias*, three leagues from Peking. The parapets of this bridge are of marble, and on each side are a hundred and forty-eight marble posts; at each extremity, four elephants, recumbent in marble, guard the entrance."

This is not the picture of a country where the working classes are in a state of abject wretchedness. Take now a more rural scene. The following is part of a letter from Father Du Mailla, and gives a description of the Chinese part of the Island of Formosa:

"The part of Formosa possessed by the Chinese certainly deserves the name that has been given to it. It is a most beautiful country. The air is pure, and the sky always clear. The soil is watered by a number of small rivers, and produces every species of grain—wheat, rice, barley, and others—also, most of the fruits peculiar to the Indies, such as oranges, bananas, ananas, guagavas, papayas, and cocoanuts, together with peaches, apricots, figs, grapes, chestnuts, pomegranates, and the rest that flourish in Europe and America. Their water-melons are much larger than ours, and are highly relished by the Chinese, although they are not equal to those of Brazil. Tobacco and sugar succeed perfectly well. All these trees, shrubs and plants, are so beautifully arranged, that, after the rice has been transplanted and set out again in squares, the whole plain has the appearance of a vast garden rather than a field."

But, without dwelling on the mere external appearance of the country, which is, after all, only an indirect, though sure test of the condition of the people, I will direct your attention somewhat more particularly to the description given by Father Jacquemin, of the Island of *Tsong-ming*, at the mouth of the river *Yang-Tse-Kiang*, (Child of the Ocean,) and the mode of subsistence of the inhabitants.

This island is not one of the most favorably situated or of the most fertile spots in the empire.   It was originally like the Netherlands, a sand-bank, and was gradually raised by deposits from the current of the river, until it became an island, some eighty English miles in length, and twenty in breadth ; separated from the continent by a strait twenty miles wide.   The first inhabitants were convicts, sentenced to reside there, as a punishment for their crimes; the place being, at the time, a mere unproductive marsh, overgrown with weeds.   By them it was gradually brought under cultivation ; and, as the settlement increased in numbers and importance, other persons of a better character came over from the continent, and the population thickened, until, notwithstanding the natural disadvantages of the situation, it has become as dense as in any part of the empire.   Father Jacquemin does not give the exact proportion between the territory and the population, but describes the whole island, as in a manner " one continuous village."   His account of the appearance of it is as follows :

"The aspect of the island is very agreeable.   The multitude of houses with which the whole   country is covered, delight the eye.   At short distances from each other, are large towns, having numerous warehouses and shops, provided in abundance with every sort of desira ble articles ; some with rich silks and other stuffs ; some with necessaries, comforts and luxuries for the table ; others with furniture and all sorts of household articles.   Between these towns are scattered about as many separate houses, as there are families employed in agricultural labors.   These houses are of different kinds ; the best are of brick, roofed with tiles ; others are made of bamboo and roofed with straw.   The whole island is intersected in all directions with canals, both sides of which are commonly planted with trees.   The high-ways, which are very narrow, on account of the limited extent of the territory, are bordered everywhere with small houses of entertainment for the use of travellers.   *You would almost imagine that the whole island is one immense village !*"

This, you will perceive, is the picture of one of the divisions of the Celestial Empire, least favored by nature, and in which subsistence, so far as it depends on fertility of soil, is attainable with the greatest difficulty.   It is, nevertheless, fully as populous as the most fertile provinces ; and it is here, therefore, if anywhere in China, that we shall find this pressure of the population against the means of subsistence, of which the British economists are in so much dread.   Unfortunately for their theories, it appears that in this case, as in that of the Netherlands, and various other parts of Europe, the most densely peopled countries are precisely those, in which the means of subsistence are cheapest and most abundant.   Father Jacquemin anticipates the difficulty, and enters with a good deal of detail into the manner in which it is solved.   This he was able to do from having resided many years on the island, which was the scene of his mission.   The passage is, therefore, on every account, peculiarly instructive and valuable.   This must be my excuse for troubling you with an extract of some length.

"You will, doubtless, inquire, my reverend father," he writes to his correspondent, "how so great a number of inhabitants can subsist upon so small and naturally so unproductive an island?   The details that I shall proceed to give you, will show you with what facility this apparently difficult work is accomplished.

"In the first place, every inch of ground is turned to account.   The land is of three kinds.   The marshes on the coast produce nothing but bamboo.   This is employed as material for the poorer sort of houses—as an article of trade with the neighboring coast— as fire, wood, and as fuel to be used in the furnaces in preparing salt.   ' You see,' said one of his converts to the worthy missionary, ' the goodness of Providence in supplying us with these reeds so nearly at hand. If we had to go to a distance for them, we could never support the fatigue, and we could make no salt.'

"The second sort of land is the upland. Upon this they raise annually two crops— one of some sort of grain, such as wheat, barley, &c., which is reaped in May; the other of rice or cotton, which is reaped in September. The culture of the rice is the most laborious, as it must be kept constantly under water, and is all transplanted by hand. The water they use is the sea-water from the canals; and 'by an admirable arrangement of Providence,' says the excellent missionary, ' this water, which is salt at all other times of the year, becomes fresh when they have occasion to use it in irrigating the crop.'

"There is a third sort of land, scattered in spots about the island, of a grey color, and apparently sterile, but which the people turn to good account, by making salt of it. It appears to be saturated with this article. They collect the earth into heaps, upon which they pour water. This running through, carries the salt with it in solution, and is afterwards boiled down over furnaces by the women and children. In this way they provide salt for their own consumption, and obtain an article for trade with the neighboring continent.

"The produce of their agricultural and manufacturing labor beyond their own consumption, is exchanged to a considerable extent, for fish, fresh and salted, which are among the staple articles of food. Very few of the natives are employed in the fisheries; but at the proper season, an 'infinite number of fishing boats arrive, loaded with fresh fish of excellent quality.' Some of these are particularly described. One of the best weighs, on the average, not less than forty pounds; another, called the *yellow fish*, resembles the cod. ' It is incredible what quantities of these fish are consumed fresh, along the whole coast of the continent, from To-Keen to Shan-Toong, beside those that are salted where they are taken. All these fish are sold at very low prices, although the charges are considerable; for,' says the worthy father, ' the dealers are obliged, in the first place, to purchase a permit to carry on the trade from the Mandarin; then to go twenty leagues into the country to get a supply of ice; then to buy the fish as it comes from the net, and place it on layers of ice in the hold of their junks, as they pack herrings in casks at Dieppe. In this way fish is transported to distant places, and is still sold extremely cheap.'

All this does not look much like absolute starvation; but "these," says the father, "is far from being sufficient to supply the wants of the *prodigious multitude* of the inhabitants of the island." Between the sixth and the ninth months they import immense quantities of salted fish from the continent. It is made along the whole coast, from the mouth of the river to Shan-Toong. Large tracts upon the shore are so arranged, that at the season when the fish from the sea or from the river frequent them, the water is let off, and the fish are taken by hand. They are then salted, and sold to the islanders at very low rates.

"The soil is not favorable to fruits, but is excellent for vegetables, of which they have the greatest abundance. From the seeds of some of these they make oil of very good quality, which is used for sauces. ' Our French cooks,' says the father, ' would be rather surprised to learn that the Chinese are not behind them in gastronomic science. Their dishes are not inferior to ours in flavor, and are much less costly. With a few beans and a little flour of rice or wheat, they know how to prepare a variety of dishes of excellent flavor.'

"The most common meat is pork: it is better than that of Europe, and is considered by the Chinese as far superior to that of any other country. Geese, ducks, and especially fowls, are very abundant, and much cheaper than in Europe. In winter the coast is covered with wild fowl, which are taken in nets. Cows are used only for work.

"There are no grapes on the island, but the inhabitants have wine in abundance, made from rice. The rice is steeped in water with some other ingredients for twenty or thirty days. It is afterwards boiled, and when the grain is dissolved, the liquor ferments and sends up a thick vapor. This operation being over, there remains in the vessel a pure wine, which is drawn off and preserved in earthen jars. From the lees they prepare a distilled spirit, equal in strength to our brandy.

"Large numbers of persons are employed in carrying on the trade, required by these exchanges; and this extensive commerce gives support to a part of the *inconceivable multitude* of the inhabitants. It is never interrupted, excepting on the first days of the year, which are devoted to visiting and amusement. At all other times there is a continual coming and going in town and country. Some are bringing from the continent an immense quantity of rice, that which is raised on the island not being sufficient to support the people for two months. Others are carrying to the continent their cotton—their clothes, and their other manufactures, or returning with all sorts of supplies, which find a ready sale. I have seen traders, for example, who, within three or four days after their return, had sold as many as six thousand cases proper for the season.

"The very poorest persons, with a litte economy, find an easy subsistence. Many families, composed of father, mother, and two or three children, beginning with a capital of a dollar or two, live comfortably on the profit of their little business, wear silk dresses on gala days, and in a few years, amass enough to be able to carry on an extensive trade. This is a matter of daily occurrence. A person so situated, determines, for example, to open a little house of refreshment; with his dollar or two in hand, he buys a little sugar, wheat-flour and rice. These articles he makes up into cakes, and exposes them for sale an hour or two before day-light, to kindle, (as they say here,) the appetite of travellers. No sooner is the shop open, than the whole stock is taken off by the villagers and travellers, the workmen, porters, suitors in the courts, and the boys, (for everybody here rises betimes,) so that before noon the shopman has already doubled his capital three or four times over, and is ready to stock his shop on a larger scale the following day.

"There are about four thousand soldiers stationed on the island, who receive a sum in money equivalent to about five cents, and a measure (about a pound) of rice a day, which is the quantity considered sufficient for a man's subsistence. They are occasionally reviewed, bu', at other times, they are allowed to employ themselves in any way they prefer; so that the place of a common soldier is a good business, and is sought for, instead of being shunned, as in Europe. There are also, on the island, about four hundred literary graduates, "*promoted men,*" as they are called, that is, persons who have distinguished themselves at the great triennial literary examination for the province, and receive a pension from the government, with a right to an appointment on the occurrence of a vacancy. There are also ten or a dozen persons who have received the higher degrees, and a large number between the ages of sixteen and forty, who come every three years to attend the examination and qualify themselves for promotion. At the head of the administration of the island is a Mandarin of the literary class, who receives and pays over the taxes, dispenses justice in civil and criminal cases, and maintains the public peace. The people, though considered less polished in their manners than some of their neighbors, are courteous, cheerful, and in general kind to each other in their mutual intercourse; presenting, on the whole, the appearance of an eminently thriving, prosperous, and well ordered community."

Here, then, is another example, precisely parallel to that of the Netherlands in Europe,—which, of itself, entirely demolishes the *permanent starvation* theory in all its parts. The island has attained the utmost possible density of population under every disadvantage of soil, climate and mode of settlement. What then becomes of the supposition, that population naturally keeps pace with fertility of soil? Again : the climate does not afford from its own products the means of feeding the people for two out of the twelve months, notwithstanding which, the supply of provisions at the lowest rates and of all descriptions,—fish, flesh, fowl, fruits and vegetables, is unexhausted and inexhaustible. What then becomes of the doctrine, that, as soon as the best soils are taken into cultivation, population presses against the means of subsistence,—in other words,—that there is a permanent scarcity? One such case, I repeat, is, of itself, a complete and unanswerable refutation of the whole theory.

It is time, however, to close this long, and, I fear, very tedious letter. I have endeavored to show, that the depressed "abject poverty" of the working classes in China, which has been adduced by Malthus and others in proof of the correctness of the anti-population theory, is entirely unreal and imaginary—" that, far from being less favorably situated in regard to the supply of the necessaries and comforts of life, than the same class in other countries,—they are probably better fed, clothed, lodged, in one word, better paid, than the working class of, perhaps, any other part of the world. It is true, that money wages are lower than they are with us in the United States, though not lower than they are on an average in Great Britain and on the continent of Europe ; but I need not say to an experienced teacher of political economy, that the rate of money wages is no test of the real reward of labor, which is determined by the amount of the necessaries and comforts of life, which the laborer's money wages place at his disposal. If the laborer in New-England, receiving a paper dollar every day, can barely make the two ends of the year meet, and in China, receiving only fifteen copper cents a day lives better, and can have, if he chooses, thirty-three dollars in the Savings' Bank at the year's end, it is apparent, that the reward of labor, or the rate of wages, is really higher in China than it is even in New-England.

It would be easy to show that in this, and all other cases, density of population, far from being a cause of comparative scarcity, is itself the proximate cause of the comparative abundance of the necessaries and comforts of life which we witness in China, and most other densely peopled countries. Assuming this to be true, the further question would then present itself, why the operation of the principle is not as uniform as it is beneficial ;—why, since densely peopled countries, like China and Holland, are overflowing with wealth as well as inhabitants, while others, like Ireland,—far more fertile and equally populous,—are constantly poor, and at times sinking into the gulph of absolute starvation ? This is the great problem that now agitates the public mind in Great Britain, and for which her enlightened statesmen are now laboring, as yet without any very satisfactory result, to find a solution. These questions have already been discussed in a summary way in the preceding parts of this correspondence, and cannot, of course, be resumed at the close of a long letter. The general answer to the second would undoubtedly be, that the naturally beneficial influences of the progress and density of population, where it fails to be realized, is defeated by the effect of vicious political institutions. So far the solution of the problem is comparatively easy. To discover in each case the particular form of misgovernment which does the mischief, is a more difficult matter, and another still harder task is to find and apply the proper remedy. The combined wisdom of all the great statesmen in England—and they seem to be now co-operating with extraordinary unanimity and good faith for the purpose—will not, I fear, be more than sufficient to effect it. The case is one of immediate life and death to half the population of Ireland, and, on a larger view, involves the prosperity and even existence of the vast future of the British Empire.

My present object has been merely to apply to China the principles which were briefly stated in the preceding parts of this correspondence. It has been a source of great satisfaction to me to find them confirmed, instead of being, as you appeared to think that they would be, confuted, by this striking and splendid example.

Having seen in the newspapers, since I wrote to you last, a notice of your having resigned the place of Professor in the University of Virginia, and not knowing exactly your present residence, I transmit this letter to my friend, Mr. O'Sullivan, with directions to forward it to you. As the letters that have passed between us on this subject have been published in the Democratic Review, I shall also authorise him, if he thinks proper, to procure the insertion of this in the same journal. Should you feel disposed to continue the correspondence, I shall be most happy to hear from you farther on the subject, and to furnish you with such information upon this, or any other topic, as may be within my reach.

I am, dear Sir, very truly and faithfully,
Your friend and obedient servant,
A. H. EVERETT.

Hon. GEORGE TUCKER, *late Professor of Moral Philosophy in the University of Virginia*